JUSTICE IN LAW

PABLO R. BANCHIO

PhD in Law (Orientation in Private Law). Master in Business Law. Specialist in Business Legal Advice. Post-doctorate in Fundamental Principles and Human Rights

JUSTICE IN LAW

Dikelogical dimension of the Trialist Theory of the Juridical World

© Copyright
Forum Accademico
Buenos Aires 2020

Banchio, Pablo R.
Justice in Law. Dikelogical dimension of the Trialist Theory of the Juridical World/ Pablo R. Banchio. - 1a ed revisada. - Ciudad Autónoma de Buenos Aires: Forum Accademico, 2020.
98 p.; 22,86 x 15,24 cm.

ISBN 979-858-69880-3-4

1. Derecho. 2. Teoría General del Derecho. 3. Filosofía del Derecho. I. Título.
CDD 340.1

ISBN 979-858-69880-3-4
ASIN B08RC8WGFR
Todos los derechos reservados
Copyright © by Editorial **Forum Accademico**
editorialperspectivasjuridicas@gmail.com
Av. Corrientes 980 4° – C1043AAW - Buenos Aires
Imagen de tapa: www.thymindoman.com

Impreso en Argentina - Printed in Argentina

Index

Introduction 7
Chapter I: Justice in the trialist theory of the juridical world 9
   1. Introduction 9
   2. Elaboration of the so-called "Science of Justice" or Dikelogy 12
      2.1 Horizon of History of Law 12
      2.2 Some preliminary axiological considerations 14
   3. Dikelogical dimension 24
      3.1 Justice as a value 24
      3.2 Dikelogical Axiology 25
      3.3 Dikelogical Axiosophy 35
Chapter II: Diachronic Axiology 41
   1. Introduction 41
   2. Diachronic Axiology 42
      2.1 Basic ideas of Dikelogical Juristic 42
      2.2 Types of Synchronous Justice 43
   3. Axiology in general 44
      3.1 The classes of justice in original Trialism 44
      3.2 The classes of justice in trialist developments 45
      3.2.2 The classes of justice in the order of distributions 48
   4. The classes of diachronic justice 49
      4.1 Introduction 49
      4.2 Governing and correcting justice 52
      4.3 Justice of departure, arrival, and processing 52
      4.4 Critical and constructive justice 53
      4.5 Colophon 54
Chapter III: Two theoretical contributions to the objectivity of the value of justice 57
   1. Introduction 57

2. The conception of original Trialism 58
  2.1 The realm of values 58
  2.2 Justice as a value 61
3. The conception of trialist developments 63
4. The concept of quantum time 65
  4.1 Introduction 65
  4.2 Post-modernity and Physics 66
  4.3 Propaedeutic sketch on contributions of Physics to the concept of time 71
  4.4 Quantum physics answers and justice classes 72
5. Synchrony and diachrony 75
  5.1 Introduction 75
  5.2 Contributions to Dikelogical Law 77
  5.3 Diachronic Axiology 79
6. Classes of Diachronic Justice 81
  6.1 Governing and corrective justice 84
  6.2 Justice of departure, arrival, and processing 85
  6.3 Critical and constructive justice 86
  6.4 The frontiers of justice 87
  7. Bottom line 88
CONCLUSION 91
REFERENCES 95

INTRODUCTION

Trialist Theory of the Juridical World provides treatment in law of the elements (facts, norm and value) that make up the triple dimension of the legal world, e.g., the distributions of power and impotence (of what favors or harms being and life) (sociological dimension), captured by norms (normological dimension) and valued (the distributions and the normas) by justice (dikelogical dimension). Partitions ("repartos") are human behaviors; norms ("normas"), descriptions and logical captations of distributions and partitions, and justice ("justicia") as value, is carried out through men in the Juridical World and allows us to assess the distributions and rules.

In this book we gather three articles published in the "Social Science Research Network" (SSRN)[1] that summarize the development of Justice in the right through Trialism that exposes them in the dikelogical dimension, elevated by its founder Werner Goldschmidt on a scientific basis (own object and method) to the legal discipline that he calls Juristics ("*Juristica*").

The complete presentation that it makes of justice from the dikelogical Axiology and Axiosophy and its insertion in the complex of values, opens the perspective of its correct integration in the Juridical World that is determined, in the last instance, by the possibility of achieving justice and the values that are relative to human beings.

We hope that its reading will be useful and can serve the debate on justice in Law.

---

[1] Distributed in *Legal Anthropology: Laws & Constitutions eJournal*, Vol. 3, No. 117: Jun 24, 2020 and Vol 3, Issue 166, September 15, 2020; *Metaphilosophy eJournal*, Vol 12, Issue 6, May 21, 2020, and *Jurisprudence & Legal Philosophy eJournal*, Vol 12, Issue 62, September 21, 2020.

Chapter I

Justice in the Trialist Theory of the Juridical World

1. Introduction

Starting in 1958, with his book *"La ciencia de la justicia -Dikelogía-"*, Werner Goldschmidt founded within the three-dimensional integrative conceptions, the Trialist Theory of the Juridical World in 1960, with the first edition of *"Introducción al Derecho"*. Trialism had its last general elaboration by its author in 1967, in the third edition of the *"Introducción"*, which since then is called Philosophical Introduction to Law, and which has the subtitle -in Spanish- "The Trialist Theory of the Juridical World and its horizons"[2].

---

[2] Werner Goldschmidt (Berlin, 9.2.1910-Buenos Aires, 21.7.1987) received his law degree from the Universities of Hamburg, Madrid, (1945) and Buenos Aires (1973). Doktor der Rechte at the University of Hamburg, Germany, 1931. Professor of Private International Law at the University of Buenos Aires, until 1986, of Introduction to Private International Law and Law at the National University of Rosario until 1976, of Legal and Social Sciences from the University of La Plata; of Private International Law and Philosophy of Law of the Universidad Católica Argentina, 1958-1987 and of International Law and Philosophy of Law of the Universidad del Salvador, until 1987. Full Member of the International Institute of Philosophy of Law and Legal Sociology. Works in addition to those already mentioned: Goldschmidt, W. (1952). *Sistema y Filosofía del Derecho Internacional Privado*. Buenos Aires: EJEA; Goldschmidt, W. (1953). *Filosofía, Historia y Derecho*. Buenos Aires: Abeledo; Goldschmidt, W. (1958). *Suma de Derecho Internacional Privado*. Buenos Aires: Abeledo-Perrot; Goldschmidt, W. (1965). *El problema de los métodos en el mundo jurídico (un ensayo)*. Buenos Aires: Esnaola; Goldschmidt, W. (1981). *Divorcio*

In his book on the science of justice, which he called dikelogy, "in imitation of the model of divine justice", he points out that dikelogy belongs to the philosophy of law in the broadest sense. Such a philosophy has a threefold aspect. First, it contains the application of gnoseology, systematology and meta-criticism to law; the analysis of the structure of justice -its axiology- belongs to systematology, while the outline of its content -its axiosophy- is part of meta-criticism (Goldschmidt, 1958, p. 9-12).

Later Trialism received numerous contributions, especially from Miguel Ángel Ciuro Caldani[3], who also enriched it with new developments

---

extranjero de matrimonio argentino. Buenos Aires: Depalma; Goldschmidt, W. (1985). *El Principio Supremo de Justicia.* Buenos Aires: de Belgrano; Goldschmidt, W. (2009). *Derecho Internacional Privado de la Tolerancia. Basado en la teoría trialista del mundo jurídico*", Updater Alicia M. Perugini Zanetti, Buenos Aires: Abeledo Perrot. His complete work can be seen in German in "Exkurs" in "*Einführung's in die philosophie der juristischen welt*", Banchio, P. (2017b: 57-58).

[3] Miguel Angel Ciuro Caldani (Rosario, 23.9.1942). Doctor in Legal and Social Sciences (1966) and in Political and Diplomatic Sciences (1969). Professor of Introduction to Law, Private International Law, Philosophy of Law, History of Law, General Theory of Law and Integration Law at Rosario Law School; of Private International Law of the Universidad del Salvador, of Political Philosophy in the Faculty of Political Science of Rosario, of Philosophy of Law and of Private International Law of the Argentine Notarial University, of Philosophy of Law of the Argentine University "John F. Kennedy "and of History of Law at the National University of the Center of the Province of Buenos Aires. President, administrator and founder of the Foundation for Legal Research. Among his works, in addition to those mentioned, the following stand out: Ciuro Caldani, M. A. (1965). *El Derecho Internacional Privado, rama del mundo jurídico*, Rosario; Ciuro Caldani, M. A. (1967). *Dos estudios tridimensionalistas (Análisis de los elementos materiales de la controversia Thibaut-Savigny y valoración de sus posiciones y Enfoque tridimensionalista del problema de las calificaciones en Derecho Internacional Privado).* Rosario; Ciuro Caldani, M. A. (1976). *Aportes para una teoría de las respuestas jurídicas.* Rosario: Consejo de Investigaciones de la Universidad Nacional de Rosario; Ciuro Caldani, M. A. (1979). *Aspectos axiológicos del Derecho Internacional Privado.* Rosario: Fundación para las Investigaciones Jurídicas; Ciuro Caldani, M. A. (1979). *Lineamientos filosóficos del Derecho Universal.* Rosario: Fundación para las Investigaciones Jurídicas; Ciuro Caldani, M. A. (1984). *Comprensión jusfilosófica del "Martín Fierro",* Fundación para las investigaciones Jurídicas Rosario; Ciuro Caldani, M. A. (1988). Reason in Law (A Trialistic Perspective), AA. VV., *Reason in Law (Proceedings of the Conference Held in Bologna, 12-15, December 1984)*, v. III, p. 237-241, Milano: Giuffrè; Ciuro Caldani,

in his work "*Metodología Jurídica*", presents a more "constructivist" and updated version of its iusphilosophical research that has prevented the theory from becoming bogged down and presents it in a position to resolve everything new in response to the challenges that postmodernity poses to the juridical world, such as bio-law, genetic management and the globalization of international relations (Ciuro Caldani, 1998c), perfecting the complex of legal branches and the displays of History of Law and Comparative Law.

For Goldschmidt, the founder of the theory, Trialism proposes to treat in Law the elements -facts, norm and value- that make up the triple dimension of the juridical world, that is, the distributions of power and impotence -of what favors or harms being and life- -sociological dimension-, captured by norms -normological dimension- and valued -the distributions and the norms- by justice -dikelogical dimension-. The distributive behaviors are human behaviors; the norms, descriptions and logical captures of the distributions and justice as a value, is realized through men in the juridical world and allows us to value the distributions and the norms (Banchio, 2009, p. 39).

Trialism seeks the integration of the three dimensions of the juridical world by complying with the requirement of purity of method so as to avoid pure simplicity, which mutilates the object of law by reducing its three

---

M. A. (1986). *Filosofía, Literatura y Derecho*. Rosario: Fundación para las Investigaciones Jurídicas; Ciuro Caldani, M. A. (1984). *Lecciones de Historia de la Filosofía del Derecho*, 3 t., Rosario: Fundación para las Investigaciones Jurídicas; Ciuro Caldani, M. A. (1993). *Bases Jusfilosóficas del Derecho de la Cultura*. Rosario: Fundación para las Investigaciones Jurídicas; Ciuro Caldani, M. A. (1997). *Estudios de Filosofía del Derecho Internacional Privado*. Rosario: Fundación para las Investigaciones Jurídicas; Ciuro Caldani, M. A. (1998). *El Derecho Internacional Privado ante los procesos de integración*. Rosario: Fundación para las Investigaciones Jurídicas; Ciuro Caldani, M. A. (199). *Los contratos conexos. En la Filosofía del Derecho y el Derecho Internacional Privado*. Rosario: Fundación para las Investigaciones Jurídicas; Ciuro Caldani, M. A. (2001). *El Derecho Universal (Perspectiva para la ciencia jurídica de una nueva era)*. Rosario: Fundación para las Investigaciones Jurídicas; Ciuro Caldani, M. A. (2001). Trialist Juridical Methodology, *La Méthodologie de l'étude des sources du droit*, Actes du VIe. Congrès de l'Association Internationale de Méthodologie Juridique -A.I.M.J.-, Presses Universitaires d'Aix-Marseille, pp. 137-149 y Ciuro Caldani, M. A. (2003). *Lecciones de Filosofía del Derecho Privado.* Rosario: Fundación para las Investigaciones Jurídicas, among others.

dimensions to one or the impure complexity in which the three dimensions are mixed (Banchio, 2009, p. 152-164).

This gives Trialist theory a highly enlightening cognitive superiority that enables it to achieve a "pure complexity" of legal knowledge and its relations with other areas of knowledge that allows it to fertilize not only the thinking common to all law, but also the complex of legal branches and enrich the "temporal" displays of the history of law and the "spatial" displays of comparative law, projecting possibilities to a Trialist theory with a "face" that integrates them together with all cultural displays.

In order to achieve pure complexity, Trialism differentiates the different deployments of the juridical world without destroying them and elaborates its perspectives separately, analyzes them individually and then integrates them in a coordinated way into a system, also recognizing the respective horizons in which these dimensions are inserted and that of the Law as a whole. With this it facilitates the development of the jurist distinguishing the facts that it tries to regulate and the relative values that are inherent to the different solutions; the logical instrument for the best capture of these last ones and the valuations of justice, the only absolute value of the juridical world with reference to which the others are submitted. For this reason, it can give harmonious answers, coherent with the general whole of the juridical world, not fragmented or contradictory between them, in the face of all the problems that may arise, and, in its case, it offers the keys for its self-integration.

This allows it to successfully face the challenge of complexity, one of the most relevant in post-modernity, in the face of which simplifications try to get the issue out of the way as quickly as possible by means of mere reductions with no possibility of success or medium-lasting projections or responses that may give rise not only to normatively wrong solutions, but also to considerations that do not respond to what we really appreciate as valuable.

2. Elaboration of the so-called "Science of Justice" or Dikelogy

2.1 Horizon of History of Law

One of the themes that attracted enthusiastic admiration in philosophy in the late 19th and early 20th centuries was the, until then, little-explored realm of values. At the beginning of the last century, it became one of the fashionable philosophical themes, and gave rise to the so-called "material ethics of values" elaborated by thinkers such as Max Scheler -1874-1922 within the philosophy of values. - and Nicolai Hartmann -1822-1950- (Maliandi, 1991 p. 30).

After the Second World War, that interest lost its validity and the aforementioned ethic was subjected to harsh criticism by neopositivist, on the one hand, and by the philosophy of existence, on the other. These criticisms were, at least in some sense, justified, but they challenged axiological ethics in bloc, without discriminating the authentic contributions that it contained, and which were not few. The case is that the problem of values, or of valuations, as Maliandi -1930 points out- must not and cannot be considered closed for Ethics as stated by the cited author (Maliandi, 1999, p. 30).

In this intelligence, also under the glare produced ethical monumental German authors noted, Werner Goldschmidt -1910-1987- moved these elaborations to the law, special analyzing - mind a value, justice, around which he built a special axiology, which he called "Dikelogy" -a word coined by Johannes Althusius- or "Science of Justice", divided into two major chapters, Dikelogical Axiology -whose object is the formal structure of value- and Dikelogical Axiosophy -focuses its content- (Goldschmidt, 1958, p. 18).

As he noted by the founder himself of Dikelogía, the science of justice awakened in the old Philosophy. Plato writes the Republic the first classic book of Dikelogical Axiosophy, where he outlines the content of a just regime, in the opinion of its author. Aristotle, to the draw the line between justice distributive and corrective, carried out the first major contribution to the Axiología Dikelógica as it delves decisively analysis is formally structure of justice. However, both authors were philosophers; and thus, from the very beginning, Dikelogy was confined in the enclosure of philosophy.

The Middle Ages changed little in this respect. The iusnaturalists continued their studies focused on the Axiosophy of Dikelogy, while very few followed the paths of axiology. The novelty of the Middle Ages is that the philosophical Dikelogy of antiquity receives a theological crowning. During the reign of positivism in the Modern Age, the Dikelogy was silenced. And when in turn, says Goldschmidt, positivism is silenced, the Dikelogy appears again in the aforementioned philosophical vestment of the theory of values (Goldschmidt, 1985, p. 29).

Considering that although the philosophical and theological contributions in the field of dikelogy are imperishable, they are far from sufficient for the needs of jurists, Goldschmidt, as we have already seen, drew up the Juristic Dikelogy in 1958, which two years later includes as a dimension of the Juridical World in the Trialist Theory of the Juridical World in 1960, as we have already said, with the first edition of *"Introducción al Derecho"* that in 1967, in the third edition that carries precisely the subtitle of *"La Teoría Trialista del Mundo Jurídico y sus horizontes"* (Banchio, 2009, p. 40).

2.2 Some preliminary axiological considerations

2.2.1 Horizon of History of Philosophy

Although what is designated by the word values as old as philosophy itself and antecedents referring to it are found in Greece or in the Middle Ages (Frondizi, 1968, p. 42), its use as a technical term was reinserted in the philosophical circulation - with economic sense- at the end of modernity, in the 18th century by Adam Smith -1723-1790- David Ricardo - 1772-1823- and others (Maliandi, 2010, p. 296).

However, these concerns were restricted to the field of political economy, due to Rudolf Hermann Lotze -1817-1881- the systematic reflection on value, and above all, his separation from the different metaphysical elements that "impurified" him in the reflections of ancient and medieval philosophy, where the concept, although not the word, - present in all western thought after Plato - , was designated with words like *bonum, perfectio*, paradigm, archetype, etc., with the same meaning as now We assign that word, which emerged from the economy, has finally been imposed on the philosophical level, that is, "value"[4].

In an age of philosophy, positivism strove to this - establish a free reality of values that make possible the rigorous application of methods naturalists, Lotze conceived the idea of values as something free reality. This conception allowed circumscribe him an area covered which want

---

[4] As the founder of Dikelogy himself points out, the science of Gadamer in Volume III by *Kleine Schriften*, maintains that Lotze develops the concept of value from the criticism of the idealistic ethics reflected between Kant and Hegel, the latter postulating that duty and values are not everything, but there is especially the substantial being of customs, the "ethic", complicated after Hegel's dialectical synthesis but which is what is ultimately called "idealism" and is the criticism from which, according to Gadamer, he starts to develop the concept of Lotze's value.

naturalist invasion and introduce, thus, the distinction between being and value with its famous tuning that values are not are, but they are worth - *der Wert gilt* - (Zucchi, 2001, p. 140).

It also served at the beginning to refute the positivist view that philosophy had no subject of its own - since all systematic knowledge was supposedly in the hands of the "positive" sciences - and therefore its only task could be to summarize the results of scientific research, and to show their interrelationships - the philosopher was a specialist in generalities. The theme of value encompassed cultural aspects of art, morality and knowledge that were not of interest to any particular science, except for what was said in reference to the economy, which concentrated on only one of its species (Maliandi, 2010, p. 296).

This introduction of value allowed to separate the cultural sciences, in germ of constitution, from the natural sciences that were already in adulthood. With this separation the onslaughts referrals positivism avoided, as the nature was alien to the value and therefore the methods of the natural sciences would not apply to a reality where the value assumed an importance of the first order. This was the task of the Neokantian School of Baden, and in particular of Wilhelm Windelband -1848-1915-, influenced by Lotze, and of his successor at the University of Heidelberg, Heinrich Rickert -1863-1936- (Frondizi, 1968, p. 43; Ciuro Caldani, 1982).

It was the merit of the German South-West School to rescue Kant's thought -1724-1804-, despite the division made by him between being - *Sein* - and should be -*Sollen*-, a key element for understanding the historical world, p. value. From these postulates, between the reality - being- and the value -to be-, an intermediate element of connection was interposed, the culture -being referred to the duty to be- complex of the realities -material and spiritual goods built by man over time-history- referring to values. This new understanding of value enabled a new understanding of culture, conceived by the Windelband and Rickert school as an interlocking realm to unite two worlds - that of nature and that of value - ontologically and gnoseologically declared incommunicable (Banchio, 2009, p. 23).

Shortly before these philosophical, Friedrich Nietzsche -1844-1900- values makes the issue alive and exciting of the time and his work there as a philosophy fully axiological, exalting life values, taking the word "life" in its broadest sense. Proclaim Nietzsche the need for "transmutation of values" that will allow the emergence of a new human culture, replacing civilization he calls Christian. Interprets the dynamic sense of history as a continuous creation and destruction of values. Such values, for him created by man, are stabilized in a table that ad wants temporary effect, as will later be replaced by another. While his thinking is not crystallized in a rigorous axiological doctrine was no doubt who converted values the exciting theme of the end of the century (Frondizi, 1968, p. 44).

These observations on which he developed the philosophy of values was enriched, as we saw, by the contributions from the sociology of Max Weber-1854-1920-, Wilhelm Dilthey -1833-1911- and Georg Simmel -1858-1918- or in addition, the psychology of Franz Brentano -1838-1917- and his disciples Alexius Meinong -1853-1920- and Christian von Ehrenfels -1859-1932- until building the philosophy of culture with broader horizons than those anticipated by the neo-Kantians of Baden (Reale, 1978, p. 118).

The "philosophy of values" not so designated simply a philosophical current, as with the "sharp trust life" or, later, with the "philosophy of existence" but a field of problems that were focused from very diverse philosophical perspectives and positions (Maliandi, 2010, p. 297) that culminated in the 20th century with the monumental work of Max Scheler and Nicolai Hartmann mainly, the most complete developers of a philosophy of value or axiology -from the Greek *axio*, worthy, which is worth-

Regarding the latter term, Maliandi illustrates, although nothing guarantees that it was inaugurated, it appears for the first time in an article published in 1890, in French, by Eduard von Hartmann - 1843-1906- who will later develop, in German, his *Grundriss der Axiologie* published posthumously in 1909.

Chronologically, with respect to this first use, it appears in the work of Paul Lapie -1869-1927-, *Logique de la volonté* -1902- and finally in that of the North American philosopher Wilbur Marshal Urban -1873–1952- , in his book Valuation. Its Nature and Laws -1906- (Maliandi, 2010, p. 297). In the Spanish-speaking world it was José Ortega y Gasset - 1883-1955 - who spread Scheler's axiological conception. In Argentina, Alejandro Korn - 1860-1936- published his *Axiología* in 1930 (Korn, 1939).

At present, Maliandi teaches us, although the noun "axiology" cannot be considered banished, and in fact he uses it, at least in a circumstantial way, it is preferred to use denominations such as "theory of values" or "philosophy of values"; but undoubtedly the adjective axiology continues to be useful to indicate reference to values, and also - which causes some ambiguity - reference to studies on values, although always different from "valuable", whose meaning is that it has value (Maliandi,

2010, p. 297).

2.2.2 Preliminary clarification

Given the difficulty of summarily determining what values are, we will follow Goldschmidt's theoretical propositions regarding legal estimation, despite considering it necessary to overturn Maliandi's following comment that clarifies in this regard that "an important and difficult problem is above all, to distinguish whether the values are "objective" or "subjective", p. that is, whether they are discovered or "created". Without going into the problem of whether or not there are objective evaluations - which is equivalent to whether or not there are values in themselves independent of the evaluation, that is, whether they are recognized or not as such -, it is interesting to highlight the fact that as both *praxis-theoria* always involve some *aestimatio* and, in turn, it can be said that throughout *aestimatio* involved both logos and the pathos" (Maliandi, 2010, p. 298).

For the founder of trialism, values are existences -beings-, while for other authors like Scheler, they are logical essences since they do not belong to the world of reason or follow its laws and are in an emotional sphere -St. Augustine and Pascal, among others -.

For Goldschmidt, values are captured for the reason that he does not invent them but discovers them - since they exist and are worth their own. The faculty that apprehends values is called estimation. For others they are grasped by intuition, since being not logical objects they cannot be known by reasoning or intellectually: they are known through emotional intuition and for Risieri Frondizi -1910-1985- and others, by experience -that Ortega y Gasset, following Scheler, he said that it was an experience of values independent of the experience of things - also *a priori* - although he lucidly states that, for example, the experience of artists and critics - *aesthetics*- does not capture in the same way because they add intellectual elements and if the presence of the rational elements is even greater, from the aesthetic to the ethical or legal plane, for example in the value utility the intellectual completely supplants the emotional since the useful character of an object cannot be grasped without a prior knowledge of the end it must comply with and the justice or injustice of a sentence are not evident at first instance in all cases (Frondizi, 1968, p. 40).

We will not enter here into an in-depth examination of the problem of the nature of values, but we will adopt an objective position enlisted in the philosophical current expressed by the aforementioned Hartmann and Scheler who assign values to absolute and a priori character and affirm that they can be emotionally apprehended and according to a "rational feeling" (Goldschmidt, 1958).

Through our postulates in the Doctoral Thesis (Banchio, 2018), incorporating time as a dimension through one of the "faces" of the *tetrahedron* or, we can think that value is "moving" along with temporality, in he seeks his true justice, even if the observer does not see it, in his own moment in the "real" display of his objectivity.

Slavery, animal cruelty or discrimination against women were never fair, although their deployments are being recognized much more fully today and not in the "times" that other observers visualized it in each "fractal" of history, in those that the Law took as "valuable" to do so with their powers and impotencies and their behavioral grasp of them.

According to Scheler's terminology, there are intentional emotional acts, such as sentimental feeling or perceiving - *Fühlen* - preferring - *Vorziehen* - Frondizi, 1968, p. 110; Scheler, 1948, p. 129) and loving - *Lieben* - (Maliandi, 2010, p. 321). To show the deep sense of uptake values by perceiving phenomenologically distinguished -following Edmund Husserl - 1859-1938- , his schoolmaster two "layers" of the emotional sphere, the "intentional feeling"- *intentionales Fühlen* - and the "sensitive sentimental state" - *Gefühlzustand* - (Maliandi, 1991, p. 67). The latter refers to the pure experience of the state, while the former has to do with its perception, e.g., a pain suffered is different from an observed pain.

On the emotional or affective state no intentional element, when refers to an object reference is mediated, that is, after the time given feeling. The reference can be of a causal order, so, for example, fire is the object that has caused me the pain I have. The relationship is established through thinking (Frondizi, 1968, p. 107).

In the intentional feeling, on the other hand, there is a direct and immediate reference to the object and this reference is not of an intellectual nature; it is there where the values are revealed to us. Perceiving sentimental is not attached to the outside through an object or representation, neither the object appeared as a sign of something hidden behind it. We capture values through the emotional experiences -*Erlebnis*- of sentimental perception (Frondizi, 1968, p. 107).

To explain the Nature of the value Scheler uses the comparison of these with colors to show that, in both cases, these are qualities that exist independent minds of the respective depositaries. We can Refer to red as a pure color of the spectrum, without having to think of it as covering a body surface, but as an *quale extensivo*.

Similarly, the value that rests on a depository with which it constitutes a "good" is independent of the depository. According to Scheler, it is not by means of generalizing induction that we manage to grasp the values of the pleasant or the aesthetic, for example. In certain cases, a single object or act is enough for us to fully grasp the value given to it. On the other hand, the presence of value confers the character of "good" on the valuable object. Thus, we do not extract the beauty from beautiful things, but rather beauty precedes them (Frondizi, 1968, p. 95).

Values, as independent qualities, do not vary with things. Just as the color blue does not turn red when a blue object is painted red, neither are the values affected by the changes that its depositories may undergo. The betrayal of my friend, e.g., does not alter the value, in itself, of friendship. The independence of values implies their immutability; values do not change.

They are also absolute; Condi are not amateurs by any fact, whatever its nature, historical, social, biological, or purely individual. Although slavery has been legal for much of human history, it has always been illegitimated and unjust, and that has never relativized the value of freedom.

This happens because only our knowledge of the Values is relative; not the values themselves, that is to say, our ability to perceive the values - consciousness of the values - Hartmann calls it the "revolution of the ethos ". Consciousness is limited as, eg, the horse's vision is limited by the earmuffs and behaves, he says, similar to a lighthouse that illuminates new areas and in turn leaves others in the dark not allowing us to see everything at once and explaining thus the reason for the variations without falling into relativism.

In conclusion, the value is not put in people, things -when they are valuable -goods- or actions by the act that estimates or values -valuation- but merely recognized. It is in the things and actions of men and not in our appreciation. Values are permanent in their valence, but the valuation - implies a form of knowledge of the real, transcendent, and knowable value - changes according to individuals, social class, education, time, space, towns and culture.

However, values are not given as qualities of an entity. They do not exist, then, as independent beings - substances - but as beings residing in another. Goldschmidt argues the opposite, and if we talk about values themselves and ask what world they are in, he will tell us that they are in the world of duty: values are something that must be done -demanding-. This consideration of the values themselves as belonging to the world of the possible that through the activity of a personal being must pass into the act, is taken from Aristotelian metaphysics to apply it in this case to Dikelogy (Diez Banco, 1960, p. 159).

In an analogous sense, although in other ways, Cossio concludes that values are material categories of future, in some way anticipating inclusion in the temporal "face" of the *tetrahedron*.

Louis Lavelle -1883-1951- sees no contradiction between value and reality and thinks, unlike Scheler and Hartmann who contrasted the real and the ideal that value is what gives a meaning to reality (Maliandi, 2010, p. 308; Lavelle, 1951, p. 33) and Jean Paul Sartre -1905-1980- maintains that value has to be as a value but not as a reality: its being is to be value, that is to say, not to be", which is why it is incomprehensible: if it is taken for being, its "unreality" is overlooked but neither can it be denied being (Maliandi, 2010, p. 308).

Courage is something, it comes into the world through human reality and its meaning is to be that towards which a being transcends his being. Polin, for whom value is unreal, recognizes that it is the principle of creation and transformation of the real. Valuation is the source of the reality of human works since only it gives them meaning and allows them to be understood (Maliandi, 2010, p. 313).

Maliandi, in his *"Ética Convergente"* develops the concept of "axiological negation" that becomes the condition of possibility of the experience of positive values or of the axiologically positive reality that is not only an index of the value that is outside the real but also of what is valuable in the real and that if the valuation may well begin in the unreal -or imaginary- it cannot stay there. While using the word value, one can speak of realization of values or valorization or axiologization of the real -to designate the product of action based on valuing -real / unreal- (Maliandi, 2010, p. 315).

Lopez Quintas -1928- tries to overcome the objectivist tendencies adapting this thought to the demands of the relational realities that allow us to see the intersection of "super-objective" realities that more than objects are fields of reality or fields -fields of possibilities of meaningful action- where values are illuminated (Lopez Quintas, 1992, p. 25) thus explaining that value exists in relation to the subject but not created by it.

In this way, he adapts the ideal of suspended thought of Jaspers -

Denken in der Schwebe- since it does not proceed linearly from one point to another but contemplates at the same time the various aspects of reality that make up each *phenomenon* - which allows it to move from a *ratio substantialist*, somewhat rigid, *realitatis* modeled on the analysis of objects and things at a *ratio realitatis* substantivist, relational, constellational, as firm as it is flexible, modeled on the study of non-measurable, non-measurable , non-delimitable super- objective realities, not verifiable by anyone (Lopez Quintas, 1992, p. 18).

We do not intend to exhaust here the expositions in this regard, but as it is stated, reality, unreality or convergence are vividly postulated and capture, from their approaches, the meaning, depth, and complexity of the axiological problem that, as a discipline of a philosophical level, remains open and with revitalized news.

2.2.3 Justice in the realm of values

Justice is a value. Goldschmidt starts from the postulate already pointed out in Introduction that values are ideal entities - they cover the part of reality accessible by reason as much as the materials do with the segment appreciable by the senses. The ideal entities can be enunciative - concepts, words- or demanding -constitute values that demand their realization-. At this point he follows Hartmann, since Scheler does not believe that values should be sought in the sphere of ideal objects, together with numbers and geometric figures or mathematical entities (Frondizi, 1968, p. 16).

It is true that the concepts of goodness, beauty, justice, utility, etc., belong to that realm, but everything axiological- does not end in the realm of ideal meanings (Frondizi, 1968, p. 105) since it is necessary to distinguish to Scheler between with concept of a value and the value itself. A young child feels the kindness and care of the mother without being caught or being able to grasp the idea of good (Frondizi, 1968, p. 105). Being a reality, then, for Goldschmidt, values are objective since reason captures them, but does not invent them (Goldschmidt, 1958, p. 77).

Based on Christian creationist genetic realism (Goldschmidt, 1958; Banchio, 2009, p. 153), the founder of trialism rejects the relativism of values and affirms that God as creator of the entire universe is also of the ideal entities, without prejudice of human manufacture due to free will caused by the distinction between natural and manufactured values.

In turn, regarding the goodness or otherwise of values, he maintains that God creates a necessarily good world - *bonus et ens convertuntur* - but a gap is made between fact and value from original sin. The possibility of free will makes human behavior only indirectly linked to God, since in the foreground it is human fabrication and not necessarily good due to original sin. He rejects divine voluntarism since he affirms that if God created values on a whimsical basis, we would only access his knowledge by revelation, but since he creates them rationally, we can discover them through our reason, through introspection, slow investigation, etc. (Goldschmidt, 1985, p. 371).

Within this conceptualization, trialism in the original elaboration recognizes natural values, which exist independently of man and manufactured values, produced by him, which places him in a game of reality / ideality because he admits the possibility of human creation, therefore of constructed ideality, although on this point we will advance later when considering the axiological complex, although we will now advance that natural values can be absolute or relative - depending on whether they are valuable in all instances or subordinate to another value - and manufactured values, insofar as they are not opposed to the natural ones, they are authentic and those that oppose them are false.

Absolute value in the legal perspective is only justice. Relative values are power, cooperation, order, utility, coherence, etc. An example of value produced authentic is to be a good football player when to do so no natural values health, utility or justice attack, and another value manufactured false, human superiority of one race obviously against river to the value justice and to humanity itself (Ciuro Caldani, 1984a, p. 37).

Justice -a demanding ideal entity then- is the only absolute value of the right to the thread of whose valuations the axiological dimension is constituted - as we saw from the Greek *axio* - worthy, which is worth -, which Goldschmidt calls Dikelogical - from the Greek *dike* - justice -.

At the time of its formulation, this theory was considered in the field of Law, as a continuation and improvement of the discoveries made by Aristotelian-Thomistic Natural Law. Goldschmidt said that this doctrine of the natural right does not consist of rules stemming from the ratio of the huma individual not -Right naturally stoic and Protestant but "just solutions to problems of distribution of goods and evils" (Goldschmidt, 1985, p. 382), with a source in cosmic nature - all nature, not only reason or human nature.

Aristotle was part of the human groupings, since man is a political being. From this starting point he arrives at concrete solutions, full of content and variable according to the circumstances" (Goldschmidt, 1985, p. 382).

The position of trialism, as we argued in *"La Noción Trialista"* (Banchio, 2006, p. 81), is considered to be overcoming because, although it maintains the existence of Natural Law, it also recognizes - as we saw in that work and as widely. We will make in another paper[5], in the examples of the classes of justice, the manufactured values to which the critical positions refer. The idea that the knowledge of values is also obtained from Religion -e.g. Legaz and Lacambra or partly Scheler- does not attack that the Law and Philosophy must resort to it to achieve it (Frondizi, 1968, p. 117).

The doctrine presents the balance in the recognition of man as the protagonist of a world that he only discovers in part, more significant than in Augustinism, Thomism and modern rationalism and also implies a broad recognition of the human hierarchy, rooted in cosmic reality (Ciuro Caldani, 1992, p. 63).

Cossio takes value into account as one of the main characters to elaborate his general classification of objects, which he distinguishes in ideals, natural, cultural, and metaphysical, but excludes it as a genre from the regional ontologies he develops. The problem of value appears indirectly in *"Egología"*, as a consequence of the fact that, as the Law is an egological cultural object, it is inscribed in behavior, which as such, implies preference in the choice between possibilities whose exercise necessarily requires values to guide it (Zucchi, 2001, p. 138).

Reale, separating himself from the traditional theory of objects, considers value as an object *tertium genus*, stressing that while ideal objects are worth regardless of what happens in space and time, values are only conceived based on something existing, that is, of valuable things (Reale, 1978, p. 103), in affinity with Samuel Alexander's conceptualization of "tertiary qualities", which explains that since the qualities cannot exist by themselves they belong to the objects that Husserl called "non-independent" (Frondizi, 1968, p. 14).

---

[5] Banchio, Pablo: "Contributions to the objective character of the value justice from the synchrony and diachrony and the concept of quantum time". *Metaphilosophy eJournal*, Vol 12, Issue 6, May 21, 2020, 1-21. Available at: http://ssrn.com/abstract=3576147.

As justice, as a natural value cannot be defined, we saw that trialist theory presents an exposition of it from its formal structure -Dikelogical Axiology- and from its content -Dikelogical Axiosophy- (Goldschmidt, 1985, p. 374).

The axiology has as its object the formal structure of value, its delimitation, the exercise and realization of justice, the formal laws that govern it and the relationship in which the criteria of justice are found with the real and ideal objects that they judge. As it refers to values, it deals with free ideality. Axiosophy, on the other hand, focuses on the contents of values. It is estimative and focuses on adjacent ideality (Goldschmidt, 1958, p. 18).

3. Dikelogical dimension

3.1 Justice as a value

As we anticipated, for Goldschmidt, justice is a value, and as an constitute ideal entity, is a value that demand its realization.

The value of justice captured as Trialist theory does in its founder's version is a continuation and overcoming of the discoveries made by Aristotelian-Thomist iusnaturalism. Goldschmidt states that this doctrine of natural law does not consist of rules originating in the reason of the human individual -Stoic and Protestant natural law- but in

> *just solutions to problems of distribution of goods and evils* (Goldschmidt, 1985, p. 382), *with a source in cosmic nature -all nature, not only reason or human nature-. Aristotle starts from human groupings, since man is a political being. From this starting point he arrives at concrete solutions, full of content and variable according to the circumstances* (Goldschmidt, 1985, p. 383).

For Goldschmidt, Aristotelian-Thomistic Natural Law is identical to justice. Therefore, there is no objection in affirming that Dikelogy begins with these illustrious names (Goldschmidt, 1985). Effectively, he adds that,

> *our Dikelogy, both in its origin as a theory of the value of justice, as in its bipartite division of dikelogical Axiology and Axiosophy, is nothing but the attempt to develop with exclusive view to the utility of the jurist, the thoughts incubated by Plato, Aristotle, and St. Thomas* (Goldschmidt, 1985, p. 383).

In no way is this a new continuation, but rather the overcoming of the apriorism in which, due to the ideological conditioning of circumstances, the most diverse iusnaturalist currents -e.g., rationalist-positivist- fell (Goldschmidt, 1985, p. 384; 1978, p. 375).

3.2 Dikelogical Axiology

3.2.1 Legal micro-axiology. Justice in isolation

3.2.1.1 Structure

Trialism recognizes that value is manifested in three displays and to the very value of justice is added valuation and orientation. The value is worth -its special way of being, its valency-, when entering in contact with the reality it values -the valued is called estimation material- and orients -that is why men induce general criteria of value-. (Goldschmidt, 1985, p. 387).

Following an example, we can distinguish valency -should be pure; "Justice should be"-, valuation -should be applied; "This death of one man by another should be sanctioned"- and guidance through general criteria -"Every death of one man by another should be sanctioned"- (Ciuro Caldani, 2000, p. 79).

(a) "Valencia". As *"valencia"*, justice engenders a duty to be ideal -it flows from a value that is an ideal entity- pure -it is worth by itself as opposed to a duty to be applied- that demands its realization -demanding. The assessment refers to the past, present and future totality of reasoned power and powerlessness allocations, which can only be addressed through safety-producing fractions. The assessment generates an ideal duty to be applied -currently- that will be positive if the allocation is fair and negative if it is unfair.

This duty to be ideal applied does not refer to any particular person -gender-, but for those who are in a position to defend a current just situation in danger and for those who are capable of remedying its injustice, there also arises a duty to be ideal applied personally -duty to act. The differentiation of both helps to not take on personally impossible enterprises and to not desert as much as possible. For those for whom a fair distribution, within reach of others, is not possible, the most valuable distribution is justified (Ciuro Caldani, 2000, p. 80).

(b) Valuation (*"valoración"*). The valuation of an adjudication as fair or unfair produces in human beings a rational feeling of justice. This feeling of evidence is intellectual (Diez Blanco, 1960, p. 205), it is not a sensation - necessarily subjective and sensorial-, it is the reaction to reasons (Goldschmidt, 1958, p. 36), which makes the estimation material of justice not the adjudication just, but the reasoned adjudication (Goldschmidt, 1985, p. 396). This feeling of justice is awakened by the method of variations -*Methode von Versuch und Irrtum*- which consists in mentally varying the real case by means of unreal modifications, in order to find out which circumstances are dikelogically important and in what lies behind them.

The case is constructed three-dimensionally as a problem by an adjudication, - sharing of power and powerlessness -, captured - described and integrated - by norms and valued by a complex of values that culminates in justice. There are easy and difficult cases from each of the dimensions and consequently in the whole, but never simple, not even in one of the dimensions (Ciuro Caldani, 2004, p. 1-2).

(c) Guidance (*"orientación"*). During the various evaluations, people come to intuit the general criteria of value, which for Goldschmidt are pre-existing, which once discovered, guide us in new evaluations. To each style of juridical culture corresponds the expression of a different complex of application of justice, whose supreme principle, for Trialism, consists in assuring to each one the sphere of freedom necessary to become a person (Goldschmidt, 1985, p. 398; 1958, p. 188)[6].

The empirical material of the eidetic intuition[7], by means of which we derive from the concrete valuation the value criterion, comprises the individual norms - multiple expressive valuations of fair solutions of the

---

[6]Both, Goldschmidt and Ciuro Caldani, quote Goethe in their works. The German text, which must be reproduced here since it supports different translations, is as follows: - West-östlicher Divan, «Suleika Nameh» -: "*Volk und Knecht und Ueberwinder, Sie gestehn zu. Jeder Zeit: Höchstes Glück der Erdenkinder Sei nur die Persönlichkeit. Jedes Leben sei zu führen, Wenn man sich nicht selbst vermisst; Alles könne man verlieren, Wenn man bliebe, was man ist* ". People, servant and lord at any time confess that the supreme happiness of the children of this land must be the personality, that any life is bearable as long as one does not lose oneself, that everything can be missed if one stays what it is.

[7] Intuition can be sensitive - external or internal - and intellectual. The latter, denied by Kant, is the immediate knowledge of something not sensible, such as that which we have of ideas and of first principles. As for the various beings in relation to which value can be recognized, two perspectives stand out: one that hierarchizes the different manifestations of value in relation to man and the other that does so in relation to the entire universe.

case - and general - reduced number of valuation principles that perform an auxiliary function in combination with concrete determinations. They are inferred from both positive and negative assessments, from personal and impersonal assessments. These general guiding criteria simplify the task of assessment, but sometimes at the cost of inducing errors by being false or inappropriate for specific cases (Ciuro Caldani, 2000, p. 80), so they must be established, as we shall see, for each situation.

The iusnaturalist currents are differentiated according to their greater attachment to general criteria - Platonic and Stoic perspectives - or to assessments, - Aristotelian - insofar as positivist iusrationalism uses general guiding criteria to which the use of the notion of "law" corresponds. For Trialism, the preeminence of evaluations leads to the hierarchization of positions that Ciuro Caldani calls "critical" -just like that- and that Goldschmidt called "iusnaturalist criticism" (Goldschmidt, 1978, p. 562), meaning with the first term that he does not directly provide solutions through general criteria and with the second that each evaluation -for him- is objective (Ciuro Caldani, 1992, p. 64).

(d) Pantonomy -*pan* -everything-, *nomos* -law that governs-. With regard to evaluation, the exercise of justice, its realization, is of a systemic character and has a pantonomic function since it encompasses all possible distributions -divine justice-, but since humanly it is impossible to fulfill such a function since we are neither omniscient nor omnipotent, we carry out justice in a fragmented way -human justice- (Goldschmidt, 1958, p. 53).

This demonstrates the openness of Goldschmidt's realism to the understanding that, without prejudice to the reality of the world, we men build it - we do not create it - through the fractions of what happens in relation to justice (Ciuro Caldani, 1997, p. 42).

The causes of fractionation come from obstacles to pantonomic function that derive from the future, the present and the past. In the present they must be covered in the case itself and in other cases, isolating the distribution of other similar ones - influences from outside - and with respect to the same distribution, dividing the consequences, the antecedents and the complex by means of cuts in the temporal, personal and real continuum and in the consequences (Goldschmidt, 1985, p. 401; 1958, p. 73).

The "obstacles" to the pantonomic function derived from the future can cause an injustice a) -*ex nunc* - from now on -, if the events are survivors to the distribution or b) -*ex tunc* - from now on - if the knowledge is survivor, but from a situation prior to the conclusion of the adjudication.

That is why there are methods of dividing up the future - e.g., *pacta sunt servanda*, clause *rebus sic stantibus*, etc. - and of undoing it - e.g. *rebus sic stantibus* clause. The obstacles coming from the present are a) the isolation of the trial from other similar distributions -influences from outside; b) those referred to the same distribution, which can come from the fractioning of consequences, of antecedents and c) of the complex - operate on the temporal *continuum*, the quantitative, the personal and the real *continuum*-. The causes of fragmentation may also derive from the past, since human justice encounters insurmountable obstacles in this regard and not only is it unaware of almost all the injustices perpetrated, but when this happens it cannot remedy them (Goldschmidt 1985, p. 411).

Ciuro Caldani illustrates this with the following example: if a man is judged for a murder, perfect justice would demand attention to the whole past, present and future of the case and of other cases, to the treatment that has been, is and will be given to other crimes and especially to other murders, to the fact that in the cause of death infinite other persons have intervened -personal complex-, that the consequences will be projected onto other people than the prisoner, perhaps that the dead person could have different levels of vitality -real complex-, that the future can show that the condemned person was innocent -temporary complex-, etc. (Ciuro Caldani, 2000, p. 79).

What is fair, then, must be established with respect to the particularity of each situation, paying attention, as methodological reassurance, to the perspective of justice of the concrete case, that is to say, equity -absolute justice-. With a view to generality, relative justice is transformed into legal justice (Ciuro Caldani, 2007).

The issues whose understanding is enriched in the light of the recognition of the pantomony of justice cover the very capture of law and the general, special, and synthetic perspectives of the Juridical World. Fractions are producers of security and can legitimately protect against various risks, according to the senses of the influences of justice to which they refer, and their excesses produce, in turn, opposite dangers. Just as security is a product of justice, freedom is a requirement of that value, and the former must become a means for the latter, so it is a matter of dividing up freedom to have the security of achieving the most significant realization of freedom (Ciuro Caldani, 1997, p. 40-41).

3.2.1.2 Classes

Although the right solution for each case is always only one, the different kinds of justice are different ways to discover what it is, at least trying to be impartial in the way -preceding way- of the adjudication since a neutral evaluation is impossible. The right solution for each case is especially difficult but achievable from the *alethic* perspective and also from the deontological one since they can and must be carried out (Maliandi, 2013, p. 197).

As we will go into this classification in greater detail, I would like at least to indicate that from a formal point of view we must distinguish between absolute justice - linking the situation to be regulated and its treatment - and relative justice - relating the treatment to be given to a problem with that given to another. Moreover, a legal justice -from the point of view of society as a whole- and a particular justice -that which is obtained from the angle of individuals- must be differentiated (Ciuro Caldani, 1976, p. 107).

Then, synthesizing the deployments that we will develop in "*Desarrollos Trialistas*" (Banchio, 2018a), Goldschmidt, following Aristotle, distinguishes species or applications of general and particular justice - according to the community or the individual- (Goldschmidt, 1985, p. 375) and this one in distributive -each one receives according to its merits - proportional equality- and corrective -regulating the relations of change - commutative- or rectifying. Ciuro Caldani extended the classification according to the elements of the distribution considered individually and, as we will see in the referred book (Banchio, 2018b).

From the subjects of the isolated distribution the justice of the distributors is recognized by consensual and extra- consensual ways, - discovered through the consensus or without it - and of the recipients, with or without respect – consideration -of persons. Related to the object, symmetrical or asymmetrical -of easy or difficult comparability of powers and impotences-, in a monological or dialogical way -with one or several reasons- and commutative or spontaneous -with or without consideration-

Related to the order of distributions are used for the subjects the classes of partial and governmental justice - coming from part of the whole or from the whole - related to the distributors -, sectorial or integral - referring to sectors or to the whole - in relation to the recipients -, of isolation or participation -referring to the objects -, absolute or relative -

linked to the form - and particular or general - in this case, tending to the common good - according to reason. In a more dynamic sense, one can consider the justice of departure, arrival and procedure and the governing (guiding) and correcting justice (Ciuro Caldani, 2000, p. 80-81; 2007, p. 23).

Justice demands that the being in the strict sense comes to satisfy the duty to be. It has, therefore, -as we deepen in the temporal face of the *tetrahedron* in the Doctoral Thesis (Banchio, 2018)-, a dynamic sense, which in its case is accentuated for being a value that also includes its development, for that reason it has to be discovered recognizing how the case must be solved according to its present reality - starting situation- and which must be the result of the solution with a view to a better world - arrival situation-. To these perspectives, it is worth adding the perspective of procedural justice, in which the dynamic is in the way of establishing what must be done (Ciuro Caldani, 2007).

3.2.1.3 Origin

Static aspect. With respect to the sources of justice, we must differentiate between natural values, which are manifested as qualities that we find in reality, whose duty exists independently of what men hold and manufactured values, placed by men and born of a duty to be established by us. Natural values are at the same time absolute -justice- and relative -to absolute values- -power, which is only valuable when used with justice. Fabricated values are always absolute -there are no relatives- but there can be false fabricated values -upper race, mafia loyalty- (Goldschmidt, 1985, p. 372). These differentiations are attenuated if it is thought that all values are constructed (Ciuro Caldani, 2000, p. 81).

3.2.1.4 Operation

Dynamic aspect. As in the functioning of any value, justice requires tasks of recognition - by understanding that an adjudication is fair or unfair -, assumption - of the due adjudication - and realization - the pure ideal that went through the duty to be applied becomes the duty to be concretized: the being that must be.

These stages are not exempt from difficulties that may require the rectification - of general guiding criteria or erroneous or false assessments -, conversion - of the distributors from error or falsehood to justice - or transformation - of unjust situations - at each of the stages, respectively.

To strengthen this functioning -in the assumption stage- it is worth counting on virtue, which can be moral -one seeks what is valuable by adhering to the value- or merely intellectual -for fear of punishment- (Ciuro Caldani, 2000, p. 81-82).

The possibility of the realization of justice is the supreme common denominator of law. However, it is frequent that lower values, falsified, are subverted against the common denominator of justice, destroying the integration that is due, and even that justice, also falsified, becomes a particular false denominator, inverted against the lower values to which it should contribute.

Every value is a common denominator of the *phenomena* that constitute its estimate material, even of the lower values that should contribute to it. In turn, it is a particular denominator with respect to its higher values (Ciuro Caldani 1982/84, p. 206- 219).

3.2.1.5 Products

The projection of justice to the social reality produces materializations, which can be personal -innocent, guilty- and not personal -prison as a place of "repersonalization"- (Ciuro Caldani, 2000, p. 82) and concepts -constitute an ideal adjacent to the real entity of first plane- e.g. duty to act, which possess greater institutionality -polices, prosecutors, cases of accident- or negotiability - dispositive norms in the social, labor relations or real rights- according to their degree of force on reality.

3.2.2   Legal macro-axiology. The axiological complex

3.2.2.1 Concept

The axiological complex of the Juridical World is constituted with justice and the rest of the values with which it must be linked in the Law. The axiology of a phenomenon can be differentiated according to whether it is related to its internality - endoxiology-, whether it encompasses the *phenomenon* in relation to others -Exoaxiology- or whether it highlights the link with that internality -Periaxiology-.

Justice, the constitutive value of the Law in which it culminates - dikelogical dimension- is accompanied by other internal values that may be inherent to it or incorporated into it. Inherent to the sociological dimension are the values of leadership, spontaneity, power, cooperation, predictability, solidarity, and order -in which they culminate- and inherent to the normative dimension are the values of fidelity, accuracy, adequacy, predictability, immediacy, subordination, "ilation", infallibility, concordance and coherence -in which they culminate-. An axiology of law in the strict sense can be recognized here.

At the same time, we can speak of an Endoaxiology of Law since values value social reality and the normative in the distributions and in the norms and there is always evaluative content in them, introduced by their authors in a more or less conscious way. There are also specific values that accompany the constitution of positive law, among which loyalty to the values of the order of distributions and the normative order occupy an important place, thus forming a periaxiology. Furthermore, the juridical values move in a complex of values that culminates in the highest value within our reach, which is humanity, so there is also an Exoaxiology (Ciuro Caldani, 1986, p. 9).

The relationship between Endoaxiology and Exoaxiology leads to consider the opening and closing in terms of values. As they should be, values are attracted to each other and in their particularities, they are often in conflict. The rethinking of the value displays and the relations between values constitute the crisis (Ciuro Caldani, 2000, p. 82).

3.2.2.2 Structure

In the axiological complex it is possible to recognize different levels constituted by the absolute values, -they are always valuable, e.g., justice- and the relative ones -they are or are not valuable in relation to the other values, e.g., power, cooperation, order-. Ciuro Caldani points out that humanity is the complete duty of our being and the supreme value within our reach that is integrated with the unfolding of the value "universality" (Ciuro Caldani, 2000, p. 82-83).

The teacher of Rosary confers on the human value a certain basic Dionysian sense of explosion of life - music, the choir, Nietzsche's dance or the world as Schopenhauer's will -, which in order to develop requires the help of special values, which are instead, especially on the higher levels, more apollonian and depend more on the "forces" of the basic human value - dialogue, the form and measure of Nietzsche's work of art or the world as Schopenhauer's representation (Nietzsche, 1973; Schopenhauer, 1987).

The value of humanity is a common denominator of the special values that it energizes and in some way balances. The special values are, instead, particular denominators that consolidate it (Ciuro Caldani, 1994b, p. 5).

3.2.2.3 Classes

Axiological complexes can have more totalizing or partial scopes, depending on the values themselves or the reality they value.

3.2.2.4 Origin

Static aspect. According to the sources that give it its origin, axiological complexes can be positive -"placed" by someone, e.g. God -iusnaturalism-, society -pactism- or hypothetical -they arise from mere hypothesiss- and theological, anthropological or cosmological. With respect to the knowledge of justice, we can differentiate positions that refer more to revelation, reason, feeling or experience.

Ciuro Caldani explains that the positive approach considers that man must be because God disposed him to be, and from there he draws conclusions, e.g., "we are because God thinks of us, we exist because God loves us" (Derisi, 1980, p. 321), and the hypothetical one considers that "if man must be" certain consequences arise. The first position often has metaphysical and specifically theological roots, the second usually responds to agnostic bases.

Goldschmidt maintains a positive complex, placed by God, while Ciuro Caldani, after passing to an anthropological positivity and to another cosmological one, reaches a constructivism that offers hypothetical support (Ciuro Caldani, 2000, p. 83).

In this aspect, Trialism overcomes the limitations of many currents since it leaves open to various possibilities the legitimacy by the origin of the axiological plexus. Within the already seen Exoaxiology, the values form a complex emerged from the highest value, the divinity that we can only recognize, but not reach, therefore, all the other values within our reach emerge from the highest value that we can satisfy which is humanity (Ciuro Caldani, 1992, p. 65).

In divinity, value is understood as perfection, since in God, Being and Duty to Be coincide. It is not a question, as is understood in other cases, of destitution but, according to the teachings of St. Thomas, that God is the Being of universal perfection (St. Thomas,1966, p. 166).

3.2.2.5 Operation

Dynamic aspect. The maintenance of the pure complexity of the axiological complex is affirmed by recognizing that values are linked to each other through relationships of a) coadjuvance -always legitimate- and b) opposition -legitimate or not according to the types-.

The coadjuvance can be in a vertical direction -between lower and higher values- ascending or descending -contribution relations- and in a horizontal direction -between values of the same level- integration relations. Opposition can be in terms of substitution -legitimate- or abduction -illegal-. The latter occurs when falsified -deviated- values in the ascending sense are subverted against higher values, in the descending sense they are inverted against lower values, and at the same level, the estimated material corresponding to other values of similar degree is assumed.

Among the relations of coadjuvance it is possible to recognize functions of impulse, purification, and guarantee. One value can drive the realization of another - e.g., to meet the demands of justice the realization of utility is increased. They can also serve to purify others -e.g., the relative legal values indicate the paths of viability of justice-. Finally, values can be guaranteed by one another, e.g., power ensures the realization of justice. Lastly, values have a certain internal projective sense - a value is realized in one aspect and leads to the presumption that it is also satisfied in others- and external -the realization of a value leads to the presumption that other values are also satisfied-. When these assumptions are false, a mirage of value is produced (Ciuro Caldani, 1990, p. 6).

3.2.2.6 Products

Although the products of values in law are dominated by those that originate in justice, there are results of the complex, among which are the products of the value of humanity, which has its own meaning, but is nourished by all the other values. Humanity is developed by health, utility, truth, beauty, justice, love, sanctity, etc. and adds the plus of the value of each man, incorporating this multiple sense to all individuals (Ciuro Caldani, 2000, p. 84).

3.3 Dikelogical Axiosophy

3.3.1 Legal Micro-Axiosophy

3.3.1.1 The justice of isolated distribution

The basic trialism in the elaboration of its founder analyzed the justice of isolated distribution and the regime. The subsequent developments due to Ciuro Caldani have allowed us to add the consideration of the justice of the isolated norm and of the normative order as outlined in the following paragraphs (Ciuro Caldani, 2000, p. 87-94; 2007).

From the point of view of its structure, the balance between the parts of the norm, - precedent and legal consequence and their respective positive and negative characteristics -, makes it possible to systematize considerations of justice.

The classification of norms opens channels to better understand the reference to the past and the future, whose balance is so significant from the pantomime of justice. Predictability and immediacy must be "for justice".

In relation to their origin, the formal sources of the norms and their complexity must be understood in correspondence with the best realization of justice, through channels of more or less flexibility or rigidity, elasticity or inelasticity and participation or selectivity as well as the hierarchy of sources between International Law and Domestic Law.

The justice of the various kinds of sources of knowledge can also be considered, e.g., the frequent predominance of sources that are merely summaries of laws is not fair to the understanding of the fullness of law and life (Ciuro Caldani, 2000; Banchio, 2009, p. 94).

From the perspective of operation, Trialism provides an important instrument for scientific control of it in the face of the still prevailing legalistic authoritarianism. In relation to the products of the norms it is important to recognize the coincidences and conflicts that can arise between the materializations produced by the norms and by justice. It is relevant to investigate from this perspective, if legislators, judges, lawyers, officials, prisons, etc. deserve to be so (Ciuro Caldani, 2000, p. 89).

3.3.2 Legal Macro-Axiosophy

3.3.2.1 The justice of the distribution order

The value of order, proper to the regime, is not identical to justice, but it can contribute to achieving it to the extent that order is directed towards peaceful justice. Arbitrariness, on the other hand, has strong ingredients of injustice (Ciuro Caldani, 2000, p. 86).

The supreme principle of justice of the order of distributions, to ensure freedom for the full development of the personality - or what is the same, to assign to everyone the sphere of freedom necessary to become a person - comprises two elements: humanism and tolerance.

The idea of humanism goes back to Chrysippos, according to which all men are related and destined to live in close community. The Stoic Romans took up this civic element and elaborated on it. Humanism proclaims that all humanity constitutes one great family in which all men are equal, but each man possesses his own uniqueness (Goldschmidt, 1958, p. 189-191).

Tolerance means that the only way each person is willing to convince others of the truth or goodness of his or her opinions is through reason and the conviction of others. Tolerance repudiates, in addition to the force or threat of its exercise, the monopoly of preaching (Goldschmidt, 1958, p. 199).

In the relationship between other values, and especially truth, with justice and humanity, conversion has, in a negative sense, a function analogous to the significance that tolerance has in a positive sense in the relationship between truth and justice and humanity (Ciuro Caldani, 2007).

The most just humanism in general is the abstentionist - leaving the individual to become a person according to his own choice-, preferable to the interventionist -paternalist- and totalitarianism (Goldschmidt, 1985, p. 439-442; Ciuro Caldani, 2000, p. 91). It includes the ideas of equality and uniqueness of each man.

Equality is related to democracy and uniqueness to liberalism. Equality of men requires that all have an equal say in the governance of *res publicae* - which is public - based on the fact that they run the same risks, and equality of opportunity, which relates to the assertion that all men have a common origin.

Uniqueness leads to organizing the shelter of the governed against the ruler. It is political liberalism, different - despite certain connections- from economic liberalism, which only has a relative justification, and from philosophical liberalism, which Goldschmidt repudiates (Goldschmidt, 1985, p. 443). The combination of both is the demolition regime.

When the rulers tell everyone what to do because they believe that is what they should do, we are facing the interventionist -paternalistic- regime.

Although Goldschmidt includes it as humanism -in its triple division as opposed to individualism and totalitarianism- (Goldschmidt, 1985, p. 440), we think that by underestimating the capacities and conditions of the person and the arrogation of full freedom of his decisions, paternalism would count the principles of humanism since it definitely hides a false belief of the powerful of superiority against those whose decisions they make - sometimes by imposition, deception or force -, which hides a lack of recognition of the equality of all men. It could be seen as a crypto-humanism as long as it is legitimated by the object.

When man is taken as an instrument of others, the regime is illegitimate -totalitarianism-. Abstentionism can be diverted with particular ease into individualism and interventionism can be equally misplaced in totalitarianism.

As for the means for the realization of the regime of justice with a view to the personalization of the individual, the just order of distribution must protect him against all threats: from other individuals - other individuals, from the same regime and from a superiority - from himself and from all "the rest" - illness, misery, ignorance, etc.

Protection against other individuals is usually achieved through contract law, criminal law, procedural law, judicial organization, etc. Protection against the regime is achieved by strengthening the individual -recognition of fundamental and human rights- and weakening the regime -division and decentralization -territorial and functional- of power and dismemberment of the economy- (Goldschmidt 1958, p. 215- 221).

Protection against the individual himself is often sought through education, inability to act, "resocializing" punishment, etc. Protection against "the rest" is achieved in the course of health services, employment, education, etc. (Ciuro Caldani, 2000, p. 90).

In relation to the constitutive modes of the order of distributions, exemplarity, to leave at least more freedom to the distributors, is in principle preferable to the plan of government in operation.

From the perspective of the classes of orders of distributions, the one that most integrates the complexity of the world is preferable to the one that mutilates it, because it offers more spaces to freedom, being preferable, for example, a universal order that integrates all the diversities of life on the planet.

Considering the origin of the order of distributions, if it is thought from a contractual basis, it offers greater perspectives of justice than organicism, despite the satisfactory standards it offers. Linked to the functioning of the regime, change and in particular evolution is preferable to conservation, which in principle is a brake on the deployment of the individual. The revolution has tearing indices and the mere blow usually means the simple subjection of some men to others (Ciuro Caldani, 2000, p. 91).

3.3.2.2 The justice of the regulatory system

Justice gives priority to the requirement of fidelity to the law as an expression of the authentic will of the community regarding the desired order of distribution and the imperative of legality, which, although not synonymous with legitimacy, contains important ingredients that demand it.

From the point of view of its structure, the values inherent in the system, which culminate in coherence, are not identical to justice, but they can contribute to it. To the extent that coherence is directed towards justice, it is valid as harmony (Ciuro Caldani, 2000, p. 92).

Regarding the classes of the normative order, given the possibility that all those responsible for the operation of the rules of a material system have to integrate its gaps, this type of order is in principle more open to the entry of multiple considerations of justice and therefore is basically preferable. For the security of the governed, the formal system that allows them to do everything that is not prohibited is more appropriate.

As for the origin of the system, the disjunctive character of the fundamental hypothetical rule that Trialism indicates reflects in amplitude the possibilities of realization of autonomous or authoritarian justice in the light of the preference of the former. The specific products of the normative order -unity, anti-juridicality, public order, etc.- can be relevant to express the fullness of the pantonomy of justice, of the axiological complex and of the regime of justice (Ciuro Calani, 2000, p. 93).

Chapter II

Diachronic Axiology

1. Introduction

Werner Goldschmidt based his dikelogical axiology on Scheler's General Axiology. Although we will make specific considerations in each specific development of the Dikelogy that follows, we will say by way of a heuristic and necessarily simplifying introduction that Scheler tried to establish general rules for all values, including justice, and thus determined the existence of formal relations of essence, such as, for example, those referred to by the propositions that all values are divided into positive and negative values or that the being of something that should be is good and the being of something that should not be is bad. Other a priori relationships exist between value matters and values themselves; for example, the relationship between ethical values and people and their acts as matters of the former. Other relationships relate to the hierarchy of values (Goldschmidt, 1958, p. 22).

In Scheler's perspective values have a higher rank the more durable they are and equally the higher they are the more extensive and divisible they are or the less founded on other values, or the more intense the satisfaction their intuition produces, or the less their intuition is limited to certain people. In addition, we find a priori relations between axiological hierarchy and evaluative matter. Personal values are higher than object-related values. Acts that carry out values concerning other people are of greater value than those that carry out selfish values. The values of acts - love, hate, etc. - are higher than the values of functions - hearing, seeing, touching, etc. - and these in turn have a higher rank than the reactions to something - being glad for something, etc. (Goldschmidt, 1958, p. 33).

2. Diachronic Axiology

We have previously stated that legal doctrine remains attached to static approaches, considering the Law, regardless of the philosophical position adopted, as a set of mere immobilized objects, whether these are behaviors, norms, or values or what, with relatively ontological criteria, is considered the object of legal discipline (Banchio, 2009, p. 27).

Even from within the Law, many analyzes of General Theory or of Minor Legal Philosophy neglect the contribution that Legal Science must make to understand the change of era that the postmodern problem poses for us and the solutions that it demands of us.

Taking advantage of developments in the Trialism evidenced in "*Desarrollos trialistas*" (Banchio, 2018a), the "legal responses" (*Respuestas Jurídicas*) can provide solutions to the fundamental problem with current existence of historical change, and social dynamic and static categories in the changing relationships between values.

Although in "*La Noción Trialista*" (Banchio, 2009) to allude to the existence of changes or displacements of the elements of a structure, or of structures within a system, we use the term "dynamic" (Maliandi, 2010, p. 30), in the following pages we will develop the dynamic perspectives of justice with emphasis on the temporal *axis* of the *tetrahedron*, taking the contributions that structuralist theories and developments of trialism have put into diachronic consideration.

2.1 Basic ideas of Dikelogical Juristic

The concepts of "synchrony" and "diachrony" were introduced by structural linguistics and also adopted by the various structuralist theories (Saussure, 1984, p. 100; Piaget, 1986, p. 43). Saussure holds that all science should identify axes on which the objects are located study: an "*axis* of simultaneity ties" (Saussure, 1984, p 146), based on relations between coexisting things that is, where excludes intervention time- and "inheritance axis" -where only be considered one thing at a time, but where are located all things of the first axis with their respective changes (Saussure, 1984, p. 147).

To account for the complexity of language issues proposed to speak of a "linguistic synchronic" and "diachronic linguistics" (Saussure, 1984, p. 149) and from there used with great free accordingly the terms "synchrony" and "diachrony" (Maliandi, 2010, p. 82).

Because it is a value, justice demands that the "being" in the strict sense comes to satisfy the "must be". It has, consequently, a dynamic sense, which is accentuated because it is not, like other natural values - e.g., the *aesthetic* ones -, a "result" value, but a value that simultaneously includes its own development (Ciuro Caldani, 1987, p. 715).

It is not, of course, a simple and static relationship, but a complex and changing one. Complexity has a double origin; the two factors that enter into relationship - the subject and the object - are neither homogeneous nor simple; on the other hand, the relationship itself is complex. The other aspect to be noted is that both factors, and the relationship, are dynamic (Frondizi, 1968, p. 152), as a quick examination of the question will reveal. However, in most cases, justice is understood as relatively static rather than dynamic (Ciuro Caldani, 1987, p. 715).

2.2 Types of Synchronous Justice

2.2.1 The frontiers of justice

In developing the exposition of the Dikelogical Juristic, Goldschmidt states that, as we saw, justice being an absolute value in law, the famous Latin adage "*fiat justitia et pereat mundus*" (Goldschmidt, 1985, p. 381) is perfectly applicable. However, the rigorous fulfilment of the pantonomic function is humanly impossible because we cannot cover all the past, contemporary and even less the future distributions. Therefore, doing justice supposes carrying out fragmentation and disintegration permanently, and although the just solution for each case is always only one, the different kinds of justice are different paths by which human limitation must obtain the objectivity - not neutrality - of the evaluations.

As several of the categories on which the social reality of the juridical world is built are also pantonomics, the "objective" purpose, causality, possibility and reality as we saw in "*Desarollos Trialistas*" (Banchio, 2018a), in order to satisfy such deployments we are forced to divide them up with cuts that in justice generate legal security and in the other categories, which are basic to social reality, give rise to certainty, depending on the characteristics of the cut lines, more or less permeable or impermeable "borders" are produced (Ciuro Caldani, 2007, p. 79).

As Maliandi points out, from the dilemmas of the bilaterality of reason (Maliandi, 1991), what is just and what is unjust can only be recognized as deployments of the same enormous web of justice.

To know the scope of what is just, it is necessary to know what is "unjust", in an analogous way to the enrichment of the knowledge of what is legal by the knowledge of what is anti-legal.

As we have already said, assessments of justice are produced according to a "rational feeling" (Goldschmidt, 1958), since it is clear that the feeling of dissatisfaction in the face of injustice has more force than the satisfaction with justice, transposing the frontiers of the divisions of justice acquires clearer importance (Ciuro Caldani, 2007, p. 82).

One of the greatest ways to increase one's own possibilities of distribution is to take possession of the situational frameworks to define the borders, since he who writes history, writes the future. (Ciuro Caldani, 2007, p. 85).

3. Axiology in general

3.1 The classes of justice in original Trialism

The latter, as we pointed out, is not a simple and static relationship, but a complex and changing one, because of the subjects and objects of the relationship and - as we will see below when we analyze this question, because in addition, each timeline could be considered a fractal of another, larger timeline, a different perception within a succession that depends on the observer and not on the agent (Panchelyuga and Shnoll, 2007, pp. 51-54) who visualizes a 'moment' of value in the deployment of his objectivity.

All kinds of justice being then ways to discover the unique just solution that corresponds to each case, whatever the case examined, we will always find the presence of both sides of the question: subjective and objective. In this understanding Goldschmidt used the teachings of Aristotle on variations of justice by emphasizing the relative character of distributive justice and the absolute character of corrective justice (Banchio, 2009, p. 87).

Aristotelian classes. According to this classification of the strategist (Banchio, 2009, p. 120), total justice - general - related to total or perfect virtue, consists of acting in accordance with the law (Goldschmidt, 1985, p.

377) and partial justice -particular- related to equality - since if people are not equal, they should not be given equal things either - which encompasses distributive justice and corrective justice.

Distributive justice distributes burdens and goods with a view to the respective merits, keeping the proportions in a geometric sense -A:B=C:D-, so that equality is respected in what is awarded according to what corresponds to each one (Goldschmidt, 1985, p. 376). Aristotle calls the proportion "geometrical" because four terms are considered: the different merit of people and the different value of things assigned to them (Aristotle, 1972, p. 137).

Corrective or equalising justice regulates exchange relationships (Aristotle, 1972, p. 37), be it the benefit and consideration, e.g., in contracts -voluntary social relations- or the offence and the penalty -involuntary relations-, with an arithmetical proportionality -A+B=C- (Goldschmidt, 1985; Ciuro Caldani, 2007). It is "arithmetic" because it finds its own type in a two-member equation and measures the damage or benefit impersonally, things and actions by their objective value "so that the equal is the middle ground between the more and the less Consequently, corrective justice will be the just medium between the loss of one and the gain of the other" (Rojas Pellerano, 1989, p. 214), analogically to how, e.g. $3 + 4 = 7$, the goods would be equal to the price or the crime equal to the penalty (Goldschmidt, 1985, p. 376).

Corrective justice, which is valid for all kinds of changes and interferences - both civil and criminal - differs in turn according to whether it is a ratio of change according to a certain measure – "synallagmatic" justice - barter - or in the medieval scholastic tradition (Fassó, 1966), commutative - equivalence of benefits - or comes from the intervention of the judge - judicial justice - a magistrate decides civil or criminal disputes. Corrective justice is conceived with disregard for people - merits -, while distributive justice takes them more into consideration - merits - (Ciuro Caldani, 2007).

3.2 The classes of justice in trialist developments

The evolution of the Trialist Theory has widened the panorama of the classes of justice, deepening the categories seen and based on them, establishing new ones that respond to the elements of the considered distribution: a- in isolation - individual distribution- and b- in groups - order of distribution-.

a) From the isolated distribution, we can recognize the classes in the perspectives of: a.1) the subjects - in turn a.1.1) the distributors and a.1.2) the receivers -, a.2) the object, a.3) the form and a.4) the reasons. b) We can do the same from the order of deliveries, that is, in this case: b.1) the subjects - in turn b.1.1) the deliverers and b.1.2) the receivers -, b.2) the object, b.3) the form and b.4) the reasons (Ciuro Caldani, 1987, p. 715; 1984, p. 40).

3.2.1 The classes of justice in the isolated distribution

a.1) Following the previous scheme, we will then see that, from the subjects of isolated distribution, a.1.1) the justice of the distributors is recognized by consensual and extra-consensual means (Aristotle, 1972), as discovered through consensus or by dispensing with it (Aristotle, 1972; Banchio, 2009, p. 87). In the first case - "consensual" - two people agree on a purchase and sale, agreeing on the place and time of delivery of the goods, total amount of the transaction, date and modalities of payment, cost of freight of the goods, etc., adjusting the whole operation to the agreement between them. In the second case - "extra-consensual" - a person gives or donates a certain part of the goods to another person or makes a unilateral bonus on the price, etc. (Pregno, 2011; Banchio, 2009, p. 53).

a.1.2) In turn, the justice of the recipients is recognized, with or without the meaning -consideration- of persons (Aristotle, 1972). It is "with respect for persons" when the recipients themselves are taken into consideration, regardless of the functions they perform in social life (Ciuro Caldani, 2007; 1987, p. 715); for example: a person suffers a car accident on the street and receives help from the public health service. As it is "no respecter of persons" when not so much attention is paid to the personality of the recipients but rather to the role they play; for example: a person enlists in the army and arms himself in defence of the country against an external attack, then the state rewards him with a special retirement in recognition of his heroic deeds (Pregno, 2011).

a.2) Related to the object, justice can be classified as symmetrical or asymmetrical - with easy or difficult comparability of power and powerlessness (Banchio, 2009, p.87). It is "symmetrical" when what is gained -power- and what is lost -impotence- resists comparisons according to proportional relations (Aristotle, 1972); for example: one person lends money to another and then the latter repays it. It is "asymmetrical" when the allocations of power and powerlessness do not admit comparisons; for example: a person who receives a sum of money as compensation for the death of his son (Pregno, 2011). The exchange can perform a more symmetrical justice than the purchase-sale and both are clearly different from the asymmetry of compensation for moral damages. As Aristotle warned, symmetrical justice is limited because "there cannot be a community of relations between two doctors" and "on the contrary, it is possible between a doctor and a farmer" (Aristotle, 1972). To overcome the difficulties of asymmetrical justice, there is the formidable intermediary aid of money that "measures everything" (Aristotle, 1972; Ciuro Caldani, 1987, p. 715).

a.3) Linked to form there are also two kinds, dialogical or monologal, depending on whether or not there is participation or discursive exchange by the protagonists - argumentation as a medium of finding justice for something that is justice (Maliandi, 2010, p. 194). In this sense, it is "dialogical" when it is sustained by a plurality of distributive reasons (Pregno, 2011), for example: among the conclusions of an ecumenical and inter-religious meeting with social organizations and representatives of legislators, the need to include sexual health and responsible procreation in national legislation is advised. Dialogical justice is more akin to private law and monologal justice is more related to public law. However, Commercial Law gives wide acceptance to monologal justice, for example, in the adhesion contract, and liberal Criminal Law strictly imposes dialogical justice through the process (Ciuro Caldani, 2007; 1987, p. 715).

a.4) In accordance with the reasons, justice can be commutative or spontaneous -with or without compensation- (Ciuro Caldani, 2007; 1987, p. 715). It is "commutative" when it involves considerations; for example, the home care of a member of a prepaid medical company requires the payment of the current month's fee, and it is "spontaneous" when it does not involve considerations; for example, police personnel respond to an urgent call from a robbery victim, who is, in turn, a tax evader (Pregno, 2011). In one class the foundations are plurilateral, as, for example, in buying and selling and swapping, etc., and in the other they are unilateral, as in donation (Ciuro Caldani, 2007; 1987, p. 715).

Several examples of the use of these categories -commutative- can be found in the classification of unnamed contracts in Roman Law according to the scheme: "*do ut des*" -doy so that you des-; "*do ut facias*" -doy so that you do-; "*facio ut des*" -I do so that you des-, and "*facio ut facias*" -I do so that you do-. (Orgaz, 1961, p. 129).

3.2.2 The classes of justice in the order of distributions

b) With a view to the order of distribution, the following are used: b.1) the subjects, specifically b.1.1) the distributors, the classes of partial and governmental justice - coming from part of the whole or from the whole (Ciuro Caldani, 2007; 1987, p. 715). E.g., 'partial' when an employer orders an increase in the salary of his employees and 'governmental' when it is tied to the whole regime; for example, if the president of the nation orders by decree a 10% increase in all pensions (Pregno, 2011).

In relation to b.1.2) the recipients; justice can be sectoral or integral - depending on whether it refers to sectors or to the whole - (Ciuro Caldani, 2007). It is "sectoral" when the adjudication impacts on some or all of the recipients of the measure; for example, the youngest of three siblings has been favored by his paternal grandparents by being invited to vacation with them. In turn, it is "integral" when the allocation affects all of the recipients; for example, a power cut that has affected each and every one of the households (Ciuro Caldani, 2007; Pregno, 2011)

Referring to b.2) the objects, the classes of isolation or participation can be recognized (Aristotle 1972; Ciuro Caldani, 2007). Isolation justice is produced when what is gained -power- and what is lost -impotence- is somehow separable from the complex object of adjudication, for example: someone owns vast extensions of land that he decides to donate for the construction of a school or even as when during the National Organization, the owners of land donated it for the railway and the local station was named after him.

On the other hand, the "participation" is verified when the power and powerlessness attachments are "intermingled" - shared - with the rest of the benefits and damages, surrounding the distribution chain; for example: the government has decided to turn a series of unused fiscal lands into a source of genuine financial resources by entering the real estate market, which is why it has put the properties out to tender for private investors in the real estate sector to sell them. The land has been occupied for approximately six years by families who have built their precarious homes there (Pregno, 2011).

Although justice in isolation is more akin to private law and justice in participation has more influence on public law. The first, of an exclusive nature, is the basis of the societal style structures; the second, of an open type, identifies community-wide formations. However, the differentiation of these areas is not absolute, and in private law cooperatives are strongly marked by participatory justice, while in Public Law there are goods in the private domain of the State (Ciuro Caldani, 2007).

Linked to b.3) the form can be absolute or relative (Aristotle, 1972; St. Thomas, 1966). It is "absolute" when it is based on strict premises of unconditional observance. Linked to universal treatment; for example: All persons are equal before the law. It is "relative" when it is based on guidelines that, without being less rigorous, provide for adaptation to contingencies. Linked to special treatment, e.g. pregnant women have special protection in terms of job stability.

From the point of view of b.4) the reasons behind the distributions in the whole regime are differentiated between particular justice and general justice.

In the former, the focus is on the good of the individual, while in the latter, the focus is on the common good, which is only clearly understood in relation to the regime (Aristotle, 1972; St. Thomas, 1966; Ciuro Caldani, 2007).

It is "particular" when it is directed towards the private or individual good; for example, the payment of family allowances to workers - with registered employment and family responsibilities - and is "general" when it is directed towards the general or common good; for example, universal child benefit, free public education, etc.

Particular justice is the main feature of private law and general justice is the ultimate distinguishing feature of public law, so that all other features of both sectors ultimately respond to those foundations.

Expropriation for reasons of public utility is an example of the generalization of private justice, and social assistance is an example of the particularization of general justice (Ciuro Caldani, 2007).

4. The classes of diachronic justice

4.1 Introduction

As we saw above, the just solution for each case is one, and the diversity of types of justice, as paths to the discovery of that one solution, at least, seek impartiality in the form - previous path - of the adjudication since a neutral valuation is impossible, because, as we also pointed out above, the subjective and objective aspects are inevitably intermingled in the valuations.

But the complexity does not end with this, because we only describe these classes statically, and we do not yet have the movement incorporated into the diversity of valuations of justice as a deep possibility of understanding the just solution of the case, and not only as part of the fractions with which the original Trialism had already masterfully foreseen them (Goldschmidt, 1985; Banchio, 2006, p. 84).

This is significantly achieved if the theoretical approaches of the justice classes allow a better understanding of the temporal development within their classification. Independently of the orientations, such as straight or semi straight, as circumferences or spirals, etc. with which the courses of time and the meanings of our lives can be represented, it is given to use two basic perspectives of understanding the classes of justice as we have already seen above: a "synchronic" one, that focuses on the simultaneity of the phenomena and another "diachronic" one, that refers mainly to its successive character (Ciuro Caldani, 1988, p. 25).

However, these two phenomena are also interrelated. What follows is not a play on words for Maliandi, but an attempt to show that it is easier to operate with two phenomena - multiplicity - than with one - unity - to better exemplify their incorporation as the "face" of the Platonic solid figure of the *tetrahedron* postulated in the already referenced Doctoral Thesis (Banchio, 2018). We will use for this purpose, once again, an example taken from Maliandi, for whom it is understandable that, from a diachronic point of view, multiplicity is a simultaneous change; but real changes are successive changes (Maliandi, 2010, p. 92).

Similarly, unity can be thought of diachronically as simultaneous permanence, although, strictly speaking, permanence must also be durable, that is, successive. Viewed from the synchronic side, change could be defined as a successive multiplicity, but this is easily distinguishable from a simultaneous multiplicity - the experience of seeing many things at the same time - for example, a school - does not have much in common with that of seeing a single thing in different stages - for example, a fish that becomes fish and then flour or oil, etc. And likewise, without a doubt, and even with rhetorical or didactic benefit, one could define permanence as a successive unity; but we continue to understand that it is one thing to observe that a certain fish continues to be a fish - nobody caught it - and another, clearly discernible, is to observe the uniqueness of this fish, which is one and not a school (Maliandi, 2010, p. 93).

Unity can, on the other hand, be linked to change: something unitary can be replaced by another instance that is also unitary, with which there is change - "successive multiplicity" or diachronic difference - without synchronic multiplicity - for example: A multiplicity can be linked to permanence, in the case of a set of things that remain identical over time, with which there will be "successive unity"-as we have seen, a metaphor for permanence-e.g. diachronic identity, without synchronic unity, e.g. a cabinet of ministers-different from each other, and perhaps even conflicting-who remain unchanged throughout a period of government.

To understand this better, we will use the cinema as a mere example of the perception of apparent movement - "synchronic and diachronic" - which also reveals the co-participation of the two factors discussed above - "subjective and objective".

As is well known, static photographs are projected onto the screen; if these images follow one another at a certain speed, we do not see static images but rather moving ones. A spectator who is not aware of the mechanism of the perception of slow movement will find it difficult to admit that the rapid "movements" of the dancer before his eyes, of the wheels of the car, or the legs of the horse in race, which he "sees" on the screen, are the result of his own contribution. At the same time, whoever discovers the contribution of the subject, could commit the error of axiological subjectivism, and affirm that all that we see is a mere projection of the subject. We could also speak of different timelines, where each one would be a fractal of another greater timeline and justice would be "predictive", if, as quantum theory maintains, the objective measurement of time depends on the observer and never on the agent that is displaces in time (Panchelyuga and Shnoll, 2007, p. 51).

The truth is that the contribution of the subject allows us to see the object in movement, but if static images were not projected there would be no perception. Perception in cinema is the synthesis of a double contribution: static images constitute the objective aspect and movement is added by the subject (Frondizi, 1968, p. 152). Something similar happens with justice, which is also the synthesis of subjective reactions to qualities that are appreciated in the object, to which one must add the dynamics of synchronous simultaneity and diachronic succession in movement (Ciuro Caldani, 1982/4, p. 62).

Let us see then if we can now - in the light of Aristotle's ideas of distributive and corrective justice seen above (Aristotle, 1972), the classes of justice considered static-minded that we have already exposed (Ciuro Caldani, 2007) and taking advantage of Saussure's contributions also anticipated - explain the classification from the dynamic point of view, of the governing and corrective justice, of departure, arrival and procedure (Rawls, 1986; Ciuro Caldani, 1987, p. 715; 2007) just mentioned in "*Desarrollos Trialistas*" (Banchio, 2018a) and add to it that of criticism and construction (Ciuro Caldani, 1987).

4.2 Governing and correcting justice

In the above direction we can distinguish a basic "governing" (guiding) justice, which is shown in relation to the maintenance or development of what is just, and another corrective justice, which - as its name indicates - "straightens out" or "corrects" injustices (Ciuro Caldani, 1982/4, p. 62).

For example, when a contract is concluded it can be assumed, in addition to the classes developed before, that the governing justice intervenes; but when the services are interrupted, the imbalance - "divalence" - of the powers and impotencies requires the intervention of the corrective justice. The same happens, for example, when a crime has occurred and the penalty must be applied, although sometimes the justice of departure or arrival may intervene as we will see below - e.g., pardons.

The two kinds of justice referred to above are permanent needs, because the dynamics of the world provoke changing situations of justice and injustice. In view of their coincidence, the idea of "constantly renewed justice" is particularly enlightening (Ciuro Caldani, 1982/4, p. 62).

4.3 Justice of departure, arrival, and processing

To be complete, the right thing to do must be discovered by recognizing how the case must be solved according to its current reality - in its starting situation - and what the result of the solution must be with a view to a better world - in its arrival situation. To these perspectives, which are dynamic by reference, we should add the perspective of procedural justice, in which the dynamic is in the way of establishing what must be done.

The perspective of formal justice can be referred to as departure or arrival, recognizing the tension between the two, or it can be radicalized to the extent that it is limited to having just what has been established by the path that is considered to be appropriate, so that the way of establishing what is fair overshadows the reference to what has to be discovered. In truth, procedural justice is an element of justice of departure or arrival, which is also dynamic, but it can become overwhelmed by monopolizing the consideration of what is just (Ciuro Caldani, 1987, p. 716).

To avoid this, the synchronic approach to justice must be integrated with the already mentioned dynamism of diachronic understanding, with respect to departure and arrival and of the process. Thus, for example, in the case of homicide, the demands regarding the situation in which the dead man and the killer found themselves and the grounds for or against their action constitute the starting point; the requirements regarding what must result from the solution so that a better world can emerge - which can include the unjust, for example - make justice of arrival, and the demands regarding how to establish what will be done with the killer belong to justice of formality. While there is only one justice, and while full justice must be found in every perspective, due consideration of departure, arrival and processing makes understanding easier (Ciuro Caldani, 1987, p. 716).

In a certain way, however, special attention must be given to the arrival, because the departure and the procedure are integrated more clearly in the full reference to the arrival and because in this way the axiological expansion and the leading role of man, mainly in the culmination of the temporal event, is better served. Now that the end of man can be a human work, and that we can change the basic realities - genetics is opening revolutionary possibilities - the interest in the justice of arrival is more urgent and must be greater.

Justice will increasingly be the construction of a better world and not the correction of a reality that will be formed in growing dependence on our will (Ciuro Caldani, 1987, p. 717).

4.4 Critical and constructive justice

Very much linked to the understanding of the references to justice at departure and arrival, it is possible to recognize two paths of justice that are especially linked to each other: critical justice and justice of construction. If, on the one hand, justice has a frequent sense of discontent, of negative reference and orientation towards reform, on the other hand, it has a sense of aspiration, of positive reference and orientation towards creation. Justice is criticism and reform of the existing world, but also construction, creation of a new world, and this is the ultimate meaning of progress (Ciuro Caldani, 1987, p. 720).

Post-modernity, which like every change of era implies a profound transformation of values, presents a justice of criticism to "negative values" that are not part of the justice of construction of the new civilization, such as, for example, racism, warmongering, *machismo*, patriotism, ideological fundamentalism, e.g., communism, Marxism, fascism and religious, slavery, sexism, hatred, exclusion, therapeutic poisoning, pollution and false manufactured values such as that of the artificial paradise of drugs.

On the other hand, justice in construction is based on an axiological complex of values such as brotherhood, unity, integration, peace, forgiveness, truth, reconciliation, where having implies sharing, knowing how not to impose, having to serve - power as service -, solidarity with the world, the environment, the neighbour, the companion, etc., where the one who believes is contagious.

In a critical sense, justice in law is linked to the silence of the victims of violence, who can no longer cry out, especially the innocent and defenseless; it defends with its awards families who are in difficulty, and who mourn the tragic loss of their children, it protects all people who suffer from hunger, in a world that, on the other hand, allows itself the luxury of throwing away tons of food every day. It punishes the traffickers who cause the suffering of mothers and fathers who see their children fall victim to artificial havens such as drugs.

With the justice of construction, it unites those who are persecuted because of their religion, their ideas, or simply because of the colour of their skin or sexual condition, and it appears to sanction the selfishness and corruption in the political institutions that lead so many young people to lose confidence in the construction of a better world.

4.5 Colophon

In the justice of departure, its "corrective" deployment predominates, and in the justice of arrival, the "straight" projection prevails. When considering "corrective" justice, we must recognize that it is never possible to totally "correct" the deviations from a starting situation, mainly because no two moments are ever equivalent, so we must be on our guard against the risks of wanting to correct everything or of the discouragement that leads to not correcting anything (Ciuro Caldani, 1987, p. 720).

At the same time, when considering "governing" justice, we must warn that it is never possible to govern everything, because what is done is always more complex than what is planned, so we must be careful against utopian deviations that want to govern everything and abandons deviations that do not want to govern anything. The adjudication of responsibility, both criminal and civil, must consider the inherent limits of corrective justice, and the models that are elaborated to build the future must above all consider the limits of governing justice. Only in this way will justice be more and more the construction of a better world and not the criticism of 'broken' situations (Ciuro Caldani, 1987, p. 720).

Chapter III

Two Theoretical Contributions to the Objectivity of the Value of Justice

1. Introduction

In these meditations we will try to make an argumentative contribution to the objectivity of the value of sustained justice as the fundamental basis of the dikelogical dimension of the Trialist theory of the Juridical world in the original formulation of Werner Goldschmidt (1985).

We will briefly explain the concept of value from which the founder of Trialism departs, his position in relation to the objectivity of justice and the subsequent developments of Miguel Ángel Ciuro Caldani (2019), with respect to the dikelogical methodology and his enlightening contribution to the argumentative possibility that we will develop in support of the objective character of the absolute and distinctive value of Law.

For this we will take from the so-called "hard" sciences, the concept of quantum time in Physics and from structuralist theories, the basic perspectives of understanding life orientations (synchrony and diachrony), closing these meditations with a "dynamic" proposal of diachronic justice classes.

The strong futuristic sense of Law, whose norms must contain not only "promises" that something "will be", but "prescriptions" of something that must be, especially for the realization of the justice of arrival, for a better world that "must be" (Ciuro Caldani, 2011, p. 96) installs man in the need of transcendence to that temporal future (Goldschmidt, 1978, p. 53).

The strategic legal responses, anticipating those changes of the "to come", whose indicators can be glimpsed in the present, can allow the Law to be at the forefront of them and not to occupy a place in the rear, behind the advances, *ex multis*, of robotics, nanotechnology, artificial intelligence, genetics, and the globalized market (Banchio, 2018a, p. 245).

2. The conception of original Trialism

2.1 The realm of values

An important and difficult problem is to distinguish whether values are "objective" or "subjective", e.g., whether they are discovered or "created". Maliandi, without entering into the problem of whether or not there are objective valuations (which is equivalent to that of whether or not there are values in themselves independent of the valuation, that is, whether or not they are recognized as such), maintains that it is interesting to highlight the fact that both praxis and theoria always imply some aestimatio and, at the same time, it can be said that in all aestimatio both *lôgos* and *pathos* intervene (Maliandi, 2010, p. 298).

By way of a heuristic and necessarily simplifying introduction, we will say that, for Goldschmidt, values are existences -entes- while for other authors such as Scheler, they are allogical essences since they do not belong to the world of reason nor follow its laws and are found in an emotional sphere as for St. Augustine or Pascal among others (Goldschmidt, 1958).

For the founder of Trialism, values are captured for the reason that he does not invent them, but he discovers them as they exist and are worthwhile in their own right. The faculty that apprehends values is called estimative. For others they are captured by intuition[8], since they are not logical objects, they cannot be known by reasoning or intellectually: they are known through emotional intuition and for Risieri Frondizi and others, through experience, *ex multis*, Ortega y Gasset who, following Scheler, said that it was an experience of values independent of the experience of things - besides *a priori* -[9].

---

[8] Intuitionism affirms that there are in man emotional intuitions through which objective values are apprehended, in a similar way as through the corporal senses are apprehended sensitive objects (Goldschmidt, 1985, p. 320).

[9] Hartmann, too, is determined to separate experience from the real from experience from the valuable, and his own arguments could be the basis, according to Maliandi, for affirming the opposite, e.g., the close relationship between the two

Without entering the problem of the nature of values, we adopt the objective position enrolled in the philosophical current expressed by Goldschmidt following Hartmann and Scheler who assign to values an absolute and a priori character and affirm that they can be emotionally apprehended[10].

In "*La ciencia de la justicia*" (Goldschmidt, 1958) following Scheler's terminology, Goldschmidt points out that there are intentional emotional acts, such as feeling or perceiving sentimental -Fühlen-, preferring -*Vorziehen*-[11] and loving -*Lieben*- (Maliandi, 2010, p. 321). To show the deep sense of the capture of values by means of perceiving, he distinguishes phenomenologically -following Edmund Husserl, his teacher- two "layers" of the emotional sphere, the "intentional feeling" -intentional *Fühlen*- and the "sensitive sentimental state" -*Gefühlzustand*- (Maliandi, 1991, p. 67). This last one refers to the pure experience of the state, whereas the first one has to do with its capture e.g., a suffered pain is different from an observed pain (Goldschmidt, 1958, p. 199).

As we saw before, values, as independent qualities, do not vary with things. Just as blue does not turn red when an object is painted blue, so values are not affected by changes in their holders. My friend's betrayal, for example, does not alter the value of friendship. The independence of values implies their immutability; values do not change.

They are, moreover, absolute; they are not conditioned by any fact, whatever their nature, be it historical, social, biological, or purely individual.

---

kinds of experience in what the German author calls "the harshness of the real", e.g., the experience of an unjust action makes the experience of value justice possible. (Maliandi, 2010, p. 303).

[10] Goldschmidt says that Hartmann distinguishes between the value of the law which falls on an external situation, the value of justice which contemplates a personal virtue and the solidarity which values collective work in structuring the law. (Goldschmidt, 1985, p. 476).

[11] Preference is a special act of knowledge that serves, for example, to capture the superiority of a value. It should not be confused with choosing, since the latter is a tendency that presupposes prior knowledge of the superiority of the value. (Frondizi, 1968, p. 110; Scheler; 1948, p. 129). One can see the antecedents cited by Frondizi: Louis Lavelle, *Traité des Valeurs*, volume 1 (Paris, Presses Universitaires de France, 1951), book I, part 2, pp. 33-91; Corrado Rosso, *Figure e dottrine della filosofía dei valori* (Torino, Ed. Filosofia, 1950) and R. Müller-Freienfels, *Metaphysik des Irrationalen* (1927), pp. 364-433 (Frondizi, 1968, p. 42).

The example to which we often resort is that, although slavery has been legal for a large part of human history, it has always been illegitimate and unjust, and this has never relativized the value of freedom.

This happens because only our knowledge of values is relative; not the values themselves, that is, it varies our capacity to perceive values - awareness of values- Hartmann calls it the "revolution of ethos"[12].

In conclusion, value is not placed on people, things -when they are valuable: goods- or actions by the act that they esteem or value -valuation- but merely recognized. It is in the things and actions of men and not in our appreciation. Values are permanent in their validity, but valuation - implies a form of knowledge of real, transcendent and cognizable value - changes according to individuals, social class, education, time, space, peoples and culture.

For Goldschmidt, if we talk about values themselves and ask what world they are in, he will tell us that they are in the world of duty: values are something that must be done - demanded. This consideration of values in themselves as belonging to the world of the possible that by the activity of a personal being has to pass to the act, is taken from the Aristotelian metaphysics to apply it in this case to the Dikelogy (Diez Blanco, 1960, p. 159). In analogous sense, although by other ways, Cossio, concludes that values are material categories of future security.

Maliandi, in his *"Ética Convergente"* (2010) develops the concept of "axiological negation" -from the Greek *axio* -dignified, that is worth-, which becomes the condition of possibility of the experience of positive values or axiologically positive reality that is not only an index of the value that is outside the real but also of the valuable in the real and that if the valuation can well begin in the unreal -or imaginary- it cannot stay there. If the word value is used, we can speak of the realization of values or the valorization or "axiologization" of the real, to designate the product of the action based on the valorization -real/unreal- (Maliandi, 2010, p. 315-316).

---

[12] "Validity depends on validity" according to the relativists: if there are those who believe, it applies to those who believe. For Hartmann the value has a validity that, although momentarily we do not understand it, it continues being, thus finding a way to explain the changes in the valuations. He does not consider himself a phenomenologist and proposes a more complex methodology than that of Scheler. (Maliandi, 1991, p. 69).

We do not intend to exhaust here the expositions on this subject, but as it is stated, reality, unreality or convergence are vividly postulated and capture, from their approaches, the sense, depth, and complexity of the axiological problem that, as a discipline of philosophical level, continues open and with revitalized actuality.

2.2 Justice as a value

Goldschmidt starts from the postulate already pointed out that values are ideal entities, they embrace the part of reality that is accessible by reason while materials do it with the segment that is appreciable by the senses. Ideal entities can be enunciative -concepts, words- or demanding -they constitute values that demand their realization-. In this point he follows, as we illustrated, Hartmann[13], since Scheler does not believe that values should be looked for in the sphere of ideal objects, next to numbers and geometric figures or mathematical entities (Frondizi, 1968, p. 16).

It is true that the concepts of goodness, beauty, justice, utility, etc., belong to that realm, but everything axiological - is not exhausted in the realm of ideal meanings since[14], for Scheler, one must distinguish between the concept of a value and the value itself. A young child feels the goodness and care of the mother without having grasped, nor being able to grasp, the idea of the good (Frondizi, 1968, p. 105). Then, for Goldschmidt, values are objective because reason captures them, but does not invent them (Goldschmidt, 1958, p. 77-78; 71-72).

He criticizes those who believe that justice is an artificial value because they believe that each individual man or each political group historically determines what is to be understood by justice. It is thus reached a relativity

---

[13] Other thinkers proclaim that justice constitutes a natural value that is objectively imposed, that is, with universal validity, on all men. This does not necessarily mean that its content consists of rules of distribution, or even that it originally comprises patterns of distribution, since the thesis' mentioned is perfectly compatible with the belief that what is absolutely valid is the assessment of the concrete case, the distribution behaviors being mere abstractions of similar assessments. (Goldschmidt, 1985, p. 496).

[14] Plato fell into the error of incorporating values into that sphere because he started from a false division of the spirit into "reason" and "sensibility". Since values cannot be reduced to the contents of sensation, he grouped them together with numbers and geometrical figures, that is, in the realm of reason. (Frondizi, 1968, p. 105).

of the content of the value justice whose characteristic can only be found in its formal structure (Goldschmidt, 1985, p. 495).

Goldschmidt maintains that, as our judgement of reality is always fractured; for us reality can sometimes appear devalued, that is why for him the thesis of independent values is not, therefore, an ontological thesis but a gnoseological one. It means that our fractionated knowledge of values and our knowledge, also fractionated of what is valued, can give rise to both positive and negative valuations; with this, the mental separation of values, of what is valued, remains gnoseological justified as his working *hypothesis* for the development of the foundations of the dikelogical dimension of the original trialism (Goldschmidt, 1985, p. 371).

Within this conceptualization, Trialism, in its author's original elaboration, recognizes natural values that exist independently of man and manufactured values produced by him, which places it in a game of reality/ideality because it admits the possibility of human creation, therefore of constructed ideality, although on this point we will advance later when considering the axiological complex, although we will advance now that natural values can be absolute or relative - depending on whether they are valuable in every instance or are subordinated to another value - and manufactured values, insofar as they do not oppose natural values, are authentic and those that oppose them are false.

Cultural values, e.g., fabricated, have material sources in the social acts of their manufacture (Goldschmidt, 1985, p. 374). It is not surprising to Goldschmidt that cultural values, always manufactured, require for their existence the propaganda and previously the launch. Relativism, maintains the founder of trialism, teaches that all values lack objective character, that is, real, since they are created by the human act that, in truth, abstraction made of the fabricated values (Goldschmidt, 1985, p. 393), is satisfied only with materializing them or "thinking them" (Goldschmidt, 1985, p. 370).

Justice -a demanding ideal then-, is the only absolute value of the Right, from whose valuations the dikelogical dimension is constituted -from the Greek *dike* -justice-, expression used previously, although in different senses by Altusio in 1617 (Ciuro Caldani, 2019, p. 20).

At the time of its formulation, Trialism was considered in the field of Law, as a continuation and overcoming of the discoveries made by the Aristotelian-Tomist iusnaturalism. Goldschmidt states that this doctrine of natural law does not consist in rules originated in the reason of the human individual -Stoic and Protestant Natural Law- but in "fair solutions of problems of distribution of goods and evils" (Goldschmidt, 1985, p. 382), with source in the cosmic nature -all nature, not only reason or human nature-. Aristotle starts from the human groupings, since man is a political being. From this starting point he arrives at concrete solutions, full of content and variables according to the circumstances (Goldschmidt, 1985, p. 382).

The position of Trialism was considered to be superior because, although it sustains the existence of Natural Law, it also recognizes the manufactured values to which the critical positions refer (Banchio, 2018a). It does not attack the idea that the knowledge of values is also obtained from religion - e.g., Legaz and Lacambra or partly Scheler - but that law and philosophy must resort to it to achieve this[15]. The doctrine presents the balance in the recognition of man as the protagonist of a world that in part only discovers, more significant than in Augustinism, Thomism and modern rationalism and implies a wide recognition of the human hierarchy, rooted in the cosmic reality (Ciuro Caldani, 1992, p. 63).

Goldschmidt, accompanying the adage *"fiat justitia et pereat mundus"* (Goldschmidt, 1985, p. 381), concludes that

> *If we reject from legal science and even from any science the research of justice, because it is not an objective subject, and therefore scientifically analyzable, but a subjective factor of political decisions, the jurist does not give norms, neither general norms (like the legislator), nor individual norms if they give margin to diverse possibilities of accomplishments (like in this case the judge, or the administrative official in discretionary acts). The jurist limits himself to show the different admissible types of interpretations and to make the rule in the illusory case that it would be univocal* (Goldschmidt, 1985, p. 386).

3. The conception of trialist developments

Having said all this, it is known that the deepening of Trialist three-dimensional integrality developed by Ciuro Caldani has modified this position.

In his magnificent teaching, Professor of Rosario has often argued that one of his most important differences with Goldschmidt's original conception is that an "objectivist" sense cannot be asserted either in terms

---

[15] Scheler affirms that above spiritual values are the religious, the last modality of values, of the holy and the profane (Frondizi, 1968, p. 117).

of the notion of law or in relation to the value of justice (Ciuro Caldani, 2019, p. 20).

His proposal consists of building on both what the law and justice "are". Since a society is constituted on shared bases referred to justice, on the basis of these "consensuses" that value is constructed and takes a slope that he considers satisfactory since he presents justice as valid constructions among those who sustain them (Ciuro Caldani, 2019, p. 21).

He also affirms that the Dikelogy is in conditions to detach itself from the metaphysical and ontological bases that the founder assigned to it, to which we refer supra, and to assume, disregarding relatively the contents, a methodological stage (Ciuro Caldani, 2007).

He is right insofar as, based on Christian creationist genetic realism (Banchio, 2018a), the founder of Trialism rejects the relativism of values and affirms that God as the creator of the whole universe is also the creator of ideal entities, without prejudice to human manufacture due to the free will that causes the distinction between natural and manufactured values.

As for the goodness or not of values, Goldschmidt maintains that God creates a necessarily good world -bonus et ens converuntur- but a gap opens between the fact and the value of original sin. The possibility of free will makes human behavior only indirectly linked to God, since in the foreground it is human-made and because of original sin not necessarily good. He rejects divine voluntarism since he affirms that if God created values capriciously, we would only access his knowledge by revelation, but since he creates them rationally, we can discover them through our reason through introspection, slow investigation, ex multis (Goldschmidt, 1985, p. 371-372; Banchio, 2018a, p. 153).

That is why one of the great achievements of the development of Trialist three-dimensional integrality is the proposal of Ciuro Caldani on the special development of the method that the author himself deploys in his work *"Metodología Dikelógica"* (Ciuro Caldani, 2007) and is what has allowed us to develop these meditations, which try to contribute, paths, or trails that underpin the objectivity of the value of justice from two different perspectives to the metaphysics of the founder, which are the contributions taken from quantum physics and structuralist theory and the consequent development of the "diachronic axiology" that Ciuro Caldani himself outlines in his "dynamic" classes of justice (Ciuro Caldani, 2007).

4. The concept of quantum time

4.1 Introduction

The first contributory element that we will develop in these meditations[16] is the conception of time from the most recent postulations of Physics, but which have their cultural origins in the dawn of western civilization, in ancient Greece, which is where man asks himself what the real meaning of time is: What is time? Is it absolute time or is it simply a subjective concept? Without life or movement, would the concept of time exist?

Culturally, this Western "man" identifies himself "temporarily" with the great and long periods of history that we already know. To the European rationalist corresponds the whole of the Modern Age, to the Christian, the Middle Ages, and to the Stoic, that classical period which goes back to Aristotle and before him the Socratic and pre-Socratic in the Ancient Age.

In the Greek villages of around the 6th century BC, what has long been known as the "passage from mythos to lôgos" occurred, an awakening of reason that is associated with the need to know why what is happening is happening.

After the first steps of this transit, when the mere instrumental reason has been overcome, as the capacity to measure the adequacy between means and ends, the retrospective questions arise, which presuppose the mean-end relationship but express, at the same time, the emergence of the causal curiosity. This, in turn, is not a mere pastime that could be dispensed with, but a vital need. If the gods govern the events on which one's subsistence and destiny depend, one must also know how to make the gods favors these events.

The *"mythos"* grows, becomes institutionalized and becomes the imposition of a knowledge that must be obeyed, an authoritarian knowledge that is not licit to be discussed. This authoritarianism, in any case, is its irrational part, while its pristine motives do not differ, at bottom, from the motives of the logos. This was verified in the Middle Ages, also in

---

[16] You can see the reverse direction in "Contributions to the objective character of the value justice from the synchrony and diachrony and the concept of quantum time", Metaphilosophy eJournal, Vol 12, Issue 6, May 21, 2020, available at: http://ssrn.com/abstract=3576147 (Banchio, 2020).

the Modern Age and remains today with many things, institutionalized myths as knowledge that is not licit to discuss (Maliandi; 2010, p. 84), dogmas as the axioms of Euclid's geometry, the point, the line, or the plane.

The first efforts for an explanation that surpassed the usual and official mythical versions schematized in abstract concepts an intuition of very remote origins found in classical Greece, but they have gone through all the cultural evolution of the West that have been able to retake, "demonstrate" or "ratify" what twenty-five centuries ago had been initially thought of in that transit.

Indeed, over time the increase in scientific knowledge has brought into question the evidence that seemed most obvious. The sky is not only above our head but also under our feet, and the firm Earth on which we walk is not still, but spins swiftly in space (Rovelli, 2016).

As we learn more about the world, we realize that the most deeply rooted ideas are often *"mythos"* due to the limits of our experience or that we are continually on the road to the "*lôgos*" and as Hartmann says, the thought of the unity of reason has always marched uninterruptedly through the multiplicity of philosophical theories (Hartmann, 1962, p. 182) that we schematized in *"Desarrollos Trialistas"* (Banchio, 2018a)[17] and that arrive until the current postmodernity in which they had a breaking point, as we will see next.

4.2 Post-modernity and Physics

In 1905 Albert Einstein in his theory of relativity realized that between "past" and "future" there is a concept that nobody had noticed before: there is not only an ephemeral and instantaneous present, but much more[18]. There is something that is neither past nor future, something that

---

[17] *Vide* the Horizon of History of Iusphilosophy with respect to time, from the Ancient Age to the Modern Age, in "Consideraciones iusfilosóficas para una nueva dimensión en la Teoría General del Derecho" (Banchio, 2018c, p. 18-24), can be seen andis avaible at: https://revistadoctrina juridica.files.wordpress.com/2019/04/doctrina-juridica-noviembre-2018-numero-20.pdf and "Notas sobre los aportes teóricos para una dimensión integradora en la Teoría General del Derecho" (Banchio, 2018d, p. 61-70). Can be seen and is available at: https://publicaciones cientificas.uces.edu.ar/index.php/ratioiurisB/article/view/567

[18] For Einstein's theory, space and time ceased to be independent categories and merged into a single concept: "space-time". With the scope of our limited conception, space has three dimensions: this means that, to determine the position

depends on distance, that cannot always be perceived and that we usually do not notice because it is so short. The young employee of the Patent Office of Bern shows that the unbeatable value of the speed of light imposes that the past, the present and the future are relative concepts since there is no cosmic simultaneity of events and that time is not independent of space (Rovelli, 2014; Rovelli, 2016).

A few years later, between 1915 and 1916, Einstein collected the monument to time built by Newton, writing the equations of general relativity. Not only does absolute time not exist, but space-time is a network distorted by matter and energy. The overturning is complete: as an absolute entity, what is left of time is reduced to the subordinate and tributary entity of matter and energy[19].

This, which for the physicists who support the LQG –"Loop quantum gravity" or "Quantum model of loops"-, as we will see later, could be simple, since they propose to write the fundamental equations without taking time into account in their scientific flat formulas, for us, that living beings first die, then rejuvenate and finally are born is very difficult, but Rovelli introduces one more concept, that of thermal time. And he links it to the irreversibility of the thermodynamic processes that cause living beings to

---

of a point, a reference system and "three" numbers -called coordinates- are needed. Or, in other words, that everybody has height, width and depth. Time, on the other hand, is one-dimensional and only one number is needed to specify a time interval. In classical mechanics, space and time were two absolutes, independent of each other. In the theory of relativity, they are joined to form the space-time of "four" dimensions: three spatial dimensions and one temporal dimension; each "point" of space-time is an event that is characterized by four numbers: three to describe the position where it occurs and one to determine the time at which it occurs. The fact that space-time has four dimensions is not at all surprising, contrary to what the idea of a fourth dimension might suggest. The only new thing is that the four coordinates of space-time appear united in the theory of relativity, while in classical physics they are dissociated into three spatial and one temporal.

[19] Rovelli argues forcefully that "we commonly think of time as something simple, fundamental, flowing evenly, regardless of everything, from the past to the future, measured by clocks. With time, the events of the universe follow each other in sequence: past, present, future; the past is fixed, the future is open ... Well, all this turned out to be false. Available at: https://www.lastella.blog/carlo-rovelli-tempo-non-esiste.

be born, age and die according to the length of life of atoms (Rovelli, 2016)[20].

Reality is a fact certified by the senses: the sheet of paper of the communication in which these letters appear is not a dream. The world is profoundly familiar to us. But this is where the traps begin. Hegel writes in the prologue of his "Phenomenology of the Spirit" (*Fenomenología del espíritu*) that in general, in fact, what is known as known is not known. The most common way to deceive oneself and others is to introduce something known into knowledge and to accept it as it is (Hegel, 1966).

Thus, as with Newton the Aristotelian physics, which began to be called classical, was closed, the scientific stage of Newtonian physics is already beginning to close. A few more years and a new revolution in physics, that of quantum mechanics, begins to be consummated, first as mechanics, then theory, later quantum physics and today physics is more quantum than physics and the previous one also begins to be called traditional or Newtonian.

Although the first great revolution in the concept of time is in Einstein's now universally recognized "theory" of special relativity, in 1908 Herman Minkowski, a mathematician who was Einstein's professor in Zurich, found good mathematical tools to understand this better by arguing that each sequence of events has its own time and the way in which they are combined is complex. Time itself does not exist at most, there is a spatial-dimensional network[21].

Each sequence of events has its own time and the way in which they are combined is complex because the events of the world, of our real world, are not organized in a large space. The fact that not everyone sings in chorus following the *"tempo"* of a single conductor according to Minkowski was also seen by Pirandello as an irreplaceable factor of humor, which is nourished by the lack of logic and order in people's intimate lives, which Maliandi also uses to describe the general conflictive structures and their relationship to ethos and which is currently perceived in the so-called "culture of the empire of the ephemeral", since post-modern man lives

---

[20] In a butterfly this process takes twelve months, in a cat five years and in a turtle one hundred.

[21] According to Minkowski referring to his postulates "from now on, space itself and time itself are condemned to dissolve into nothing more than shadows, and only a kind of conjunction of the two will retain an independent reality: space-time".

linked to the fleeting. Time fractures in an infinity of presents that follow each other without apparent connection (Maliandi, 2010, p. 81)[22].

Here too, the effect is a further degradation of the ontological state of time. On a microscopic scale, in fact, space-time ceases to be a continuous, albeit fluctuating, network and becomes the realm of discontinuity. A kind of foam, the foam of space-time.

The last stop, again with the acceleration of history less than a century later, occurs in the already advanced equations of the "loop quantum gravity model", with which Carlo Rovelli, Lee Smolin, and others, attempt to unify the general relativity of Einstein's quantum mechanics and time disappears. What exists on the fundamental level are only "space atoms". The universe and its history are nothing more than ways in which these "space atoms" are arranged.

In *"La realidad no es cómo aparece"* is where Rovelli develops the already anticipated concept of thermal time, linking it to the irreversibility of thermodynamic processes that make living beings born, age and die, as we said.

We can say that the time that we perceive more than an illusion is an emergent property, which appears on the scene with all its reality and irreversibility only in the presence of large sets of "space atoms", just as liquidity is, for example, an emergent property of a large set of water molecules, human beings, since it is our nature, we are beings who live in time. We do not live at the primary level of the world: we live in its complexity (Rovelli, 2016; Rovelli, 2014).

With the arrival of man in space, in 1950 the evolution of our image of the world affected the intuition of time -an illusion of the senses in the terms seen in Parmenides- and we learned that time does not pass at the same speed for everyone, e.g., it passes more quickly in the mountains than in the plains. The Italian physicist, following the paradox of Hawking's twins, gives us the example that two schoolmates continue being contemporaries only if they remain one next to the other, otherwise, when they meet again

---

[22] Maliandi uses the Italian playwright "Order? Coherence? but we have within us four, five souls that fight among themselves: the instinctive soul, the moral soul, the affective soul, the social soul. And as one or the other dominates, our conscience takes a position; and we consider valid and sincere that fictitious interpretation of ourselves, of our interior being that we ignore, because it never manifests itself entirely, but sometimes in one way, sometimes in another, as the cases of life demand" (Maliandi, 2010, p. 81).

they will no longer have the same age (Rovelli, 2014)[23], because for the time-space theory of relativity there does not exist a unique absolute time, but each individual has his own personal measure of time, measure that depends on where he is and how he moves (Hawking, 1987, p. 38).

Today there are precise clocks with which this variability in time is easily measured. By virtue of this precision, Rovelli points out, while in Genoa, on the sea, an hour passes, in L'Aquila, seven hundred meters higher, an hour and a millionth of a second passes. Not enough to influence our daily lives, but enough to show us that the conception of time passing uniformly, the same for everyone, is only an approximation due to the imprecision of our perceptions (Rovelli, 2016), an illusion of the senses, in the terms of the "eleatic return" twenty-five centuries later.

So far, we are in a well-known field of physics: the dependence of time on altitude, for example, is an effect already understood, described by the theory of general relativity, Einstein's theory and the one that provides us with the best conceptual framework, at present, to think about space and time. Again, contra factum non argumentum est. That measured effect is often considered in technological applications, e.g., the current global positioning systems -GPS- work taking into account that the clocks of satellites go faster than those of the Earth and by the difference of "time" it is possible to know where we are. We are in the field of a science that is perhaps still little known by a wide public of law, but for some time now it has been evident to specialists that in the following point we will try to briefly introduce it.

---

[23] For Rovelli, how long this "neither past nor future" lasts depends on the distance. For example, if we are talking in the same room, the range that is neither the past nor the future is just a few nanoseconds away, that is, very little, and he notices it. If it is called from New York it lasts a millisecond, still too little to notice, but if I am on Earth, and the reader-of this Thesis- is on Mars, then the 'there is a past and there is no future' lasts fifteen minutes and this is to be noticed. Therefore, you cannot have a simple conversation between Mars and Earth: because even if I try to answer as soon as I hear the question, you will still have my answer after fifteen minutes. Those fifteen minutes are neither in my past nor in my future. They are in the "in- between zone". Today any university physics student learns all this without difficulty. But the consequences are important. It means we cannot say "that's the way things are in this universe". There is no such thing as "this moment" in the universe.

4.3 Propaedeutic sketch on contributions of Physics to the concept of time

As the philosophical thirst of Western maritime culture for knowledge does not stop, research continues and although this is only a rough outline of description on which we will not develop the key issue, I would like, at least, to leave it indicated.

One of the biggest open problems is that of quantum gravity, and on which an important part of current theoretical research is focusing, is the tiny quantum structure, granular, probabilistic, that space itself must have, but obviously, as we have already pointed out, it exceeds this work and my knowledge.

What does physics understand when it talks about the weather? To know the time, that is, to measure time, we can observe the position of the Sun in the sky. To be more accurate, we look at a clock. The position of the hands on the clock indicates the time that has passed. But how do I know if my watch really measures "real" time? I can check it with the exact time issued by an official institute, where there is a very precise clock. But how do I know if that clock measures "real" time? I compare it with another clock. Clearly, there is a problem. All that we "observe" are clock hands, moving objects, the position of the Sun in the sky. We never see "real time." We see only moving objects (Rovelli, 2014).

The scientific nature of the social sciences has always been discussed due to the lack of accuracy in their results, however, the so-called "hard" sciences have also been modifying their postulates.

Rovelli rightly writes that the answers of the natural sciences are not credible because they are definitive: they are credible because they are the best we have today, at a given moment in the real history of our knowledge. It is precisely because we know that we do not consider them definitive that they continue to improve. In light of these considerations, studying Einstein does not mean erasing completely the classical mechanics of Galileo and Newton, just as studying Kepler and Copernicus does not mean condemning the physics of Aristotle and Anaximander (Bianchi, 2015 b, par. 7).

A brief history of the physics of time shows that philosophy predicted in the various already repeated examples of the "eleatic return". Although history is based on a "retrospective" vision, it must also have a certain "prospective" vision, that is, the vision of the future, of the outlook towards the future. If we were to think that we could speak of different time lines, each one of which would be a fractal of another greater time line, philosophy would be "predictive", if, as we maintain, also for the consideration of the value of justice in Law, the objective measurement of time depends on the "observer", never of the agent that moves in time (Panchelyuga and Shnoll, 2007), with inverse historiographic sense in the philosophical scope was described precisely the present time, "temporarily" centuries ago and that "now" science has verified empirically through the advances explained here.

A story of "eleatic return" that begins, in fact, with Newton. It follows a rather linear path which, to say it with the physicist and philosopher Massimo Pauri, consists in the continuous degradation of the ontological state of time. To arrive at a conclusion now, the same as Parmenides twenty-five centuries later: And this seems to have a forceful conclusion for some quantum physicists even if, it must be said, they admit that it is not yet definitive, that time is, in fact, an illusion of the senses (Rovelli, 2014).

For nineteen centuries Physics, which, as we said, came to be called classical or Aristotelian when Newton, to build "his" physics imagined the possibility of an immense empty space where time passes, even if there is nothing and nothing happen. Newton separated time from world events. He imagined that time passes by itself, independently of everything else. Like a comedy in which there is the first act, the second act, the third act, but nothing happens on the stage. Newton's time is an absolute time, independent of cosmic matter.

General relativity took another important step away from Newton's conception of time - time passes even when nothing happens. The theory seems to live another "eleatic return" and returns to Aristotle's conception: there is no time alone. What we call "time" is only a way of considering how things move. Quantum mechanics and the theories connected to it describe it as a kind of "foam".

4.4 Quantum physics answers and justice classes

We can still affirm the impossibility of certain and definitive answers to these important questions with which we began the previous point of these meditations. If, on the one hand, time is at the center of philosophical controversies, on the other hand, it has always been the point of support that allows balance - at least, what it pretends to be - in many physical equations, which man has put at the base of his knowledge of the world and of reality. This perfect mixture of Philosophy and Physics, however, has not yet assumed a definitive consistency and form and this is perhaps the reason why the "concept of time", surrounded by a mysterious fog that prevents a clear reading, remains a very fascinating and convincing challenge for many physicists and philosophers (Greco, 2014).

While Minkowski claims that the events of the world are not organized in a large space and do not follow the "*tempo*" of a single driver, in contagion, each sequence of events has its own time. Therefore, general relativity has taken an important step forward in comparison with Newton's conception of time.

Rovelli, however, states that: "in general, relativity disappeared from 'universal' time, but basically every moving object had its time, like Newtonian time: a bit like the fact that as long as we stay in Italy, we don't have to worry about changing the time of the clock. due to time zones. But quantum mechanics tells us that even this "local" time does not work at all. The reason is that with quantum mechanics it has been discovered that all physical quantities are always "imprecise", "floating". Even local time, on a small scale, instead of being like a simple line, is like a sign that has thickness and breaks into small marks. Space and time break up into a kind of "microscopic foam" (Rovelli, 2014).

In the light of these considerations, the aforementioned theory of loop quantum gravity was born, which today admits that such time does not exist - thus returning to Kant's ideas. "Because the concept of time, once we understand that it depends on things that happen, that it is mixed with space, that it is subject to quantum fluctuations, etc., becomes something that has nothing to do with our simple intuition of time, and in general, it becomes a useless concept. The theory describes how things move with each other, and there is really no need to talk about time. By forgetting about time, everything becomes simpler. It is easier to understand how the world works at the fundamental level" (Rovelli, 2014; 2016).

While it is striking that for these postulates time does not exist, this does not mean that there is no time in our daily lives, but that time is not a useful concept when studying the more general structures of the world. Perhaps, therefore, time corresponds to our way of seeing things and is no longer part of the fundamental structure of the universe. If that were the case, the physical supporters of the LQG –"Loop quantum gravity"- propose writing the fundamental equations without taking time into account. Therefore, one would have an image of the world, where objects and phenomena move in an anarchic way without an absolute time that marks and orders them. Our time is only an approximation of the many variables that occur at the microscopic level.

Paradoxically, it seems that Kant has intuited on a philosophical level an important concept: time is in fact a merely subjective and phenomenological coordinate. Thus, the concept of absolute and infinite time in Newtonian physics collapses and would not be a *"noumeno"* but a postulate, the fourth in practical reason. The aforementioned Pauri, seems to provide the synthesis of these ideas, arguing that modern physics has constantly degraded time in its history: from an absolute and incorruptible entity to a mere illusion devoid of any physical reality (Rovelli, 2014; 2016).

Rovelli says that at the bottom of the quantum universe there is the spinning movement of elementary particles that give life to infinite events (Rovelli, 2016). Other physicists, such as Julian Barbour, who lives in Oxfordshire in a house that has remained stable in time until 1689, the year it was built, think that in the end reality still "is" and write that the quantum universe is probably static, and the movement and apparent flow of time could be nothing more than very well-structured illusions". Here the discourse becomes abysmal and one would have to ask Plato about this "liquid" postulate of Rovelli, as if he were a highly refined atomist, but time is just what is missing (Greco, 2014).

As Madile maintains, it is worth saying that simple experience is life that is not reduced to the organic of the body, I transcend myself by proposing ends and projecting myself into them. I make myself, in them. But they are in the future and the future still isn't, am I, therefore, being that the time of my conscious existence is this passing that advances itself, retaining in turn a past that I need to locate myself in my present? And being that I would be giving meaning to my life, just now, this only possible future that I propose? Or could it be that my freedom begins precisely when I refuse an invariable Being and then, not being forever, it is that I always renew myself? units of life with some meaning for us; beings with "temporality"; that is: with the quality of temporaries because they have a measure of time (Madile, 2007).

Strictly speaking, we are timed rather than being timed. And time itself is not. Even in relation to movement and change, there is only becoming. As for our temporality, as a consciousness or measure of time, as a present it is not since we cannot retain it; as a past it is no longer; and as a future it is not yet either.

The review of the western thought of the preceding paragraphs inclines to think, having reached the level of complete immanence that indicates the treatment of the individual human existence as only temporization, to have reached an unappealable instance. In that everything depends, exclusively, on each one of us. That is why postmodernity, where being is implemented, materializes those aspirations, and has achieved exactly that dematerialization of time and space, which we consider that the Law must assume and solve with juridical answers based on justice, must be full of discipline. Perhaps the developments of quantum physics will install it as logos and it will be with time an indisputable knowledge, a new step of the "transit from *mythos* to *lôgos*".

It is in this intelligence that we proposed its integration as a dimensional "face" of Law in a General Theory that would place it in that vision of "observer" of a certain "time" in a specific area within the dikelogical dimension of legal science that would maintain its objective unity in the face of the disruptive "timeless" changes that it would be facing with its timeless dikelogical objectivities, captured in normative "times" "present" that accompany the social time lived but assuring the transcendence of the Law in front of them and the objective immanence of the value of justice.

This is because the agent would only observe a fractal of a determined time (that of its observation), not being able to do it - due to the arguments exposed - with the whole real dimension of the objective value. Therefore, any construction cannot be fully validated dikelogically because of its partial character reduced to its small and limited temporospatial fractal, constituting a simple fractioning of the value to which all its magnitude of demanding ideal entity cannot be attributed.

5. Synchrony and diachrony

5.1 Introduction

Goldschmidt had developed, to verify the formal structure of justice, its relationship with the legal system and the order of behavior, some methods to discover the objectivity of value (Goldschmidt, 1958).

Among them are those of stigmatic and conspective intuition, the feeling of evidence, the method of variations and the method of fractionation (Banchio, 2007, p. 13).

Ciuro Caldani enriched the ways to discover justice with the development of the constitutive methods of the classes of justice of the distributions and the regime in the material, spatial, temporal and personal diversities18[24] as paths to arrive at it and to discover the objectivity of value, independently of the subjectivities of the observer that constitute a very enriching theoretical and speculative methodology (Ciuro Caldani, 2007, p. 9).

If we incorporate, in these meditations, the dynamic perspectives of the concept of time seen before, the synchrony and diachrony will help us to better understand that the observer could not "build" a justice because that creation, both personal and temporal and spatial, would not have more validity than the one attributed to it by the subjectivity of its builders.

Thus, we can speak of a diachrony and synchrony that, added to the concept of the quantum observer that we have already seen, help us to think that it is this one who "sees" a certain fractioning of justice, like the examples of the color that we have already pointed out above, as long as the value of immutable justice does not move from its axis.

It is the valuation of the observer at a given point on the temporal axis that qualifies as "justice" something that is simply a spatially fractioned distribution of that pantomime value, in Goldschmidt's terms, guided by the general criteria of value that is formed in that specific temporal-cultural space without it altering the universal and therefore objective concept of justice, independent of the historical-cultural situation and therefore also temporal and spatial.

Taking advantage then of the wealth of the conception of *"Metodología Dikelogica"* (Ciuro Caldani, 2007, p. 36) we contribute with the idea of "diachrony", "synchrony" and space-time to demonstrate that justice is not a relative construct, but always remains unalterable, although in a fractal of another greater timeline, in a determined temporary and physical moment it is perceived in a diverse way and, the adjudication perceived as "fair" really is not.

Society could, as in fact it has been doing throughout the history of mankind, have totally wrong conceptions of what "is" fair, and this would make the scientific protagonist of our discipline illusory.

The activity of the jurist would then consist, as Goldschmidt says,

---

[24] The apprehension of the complexity of life deserves a different treatment of the classes of justice, the relations between values and justice of isolated distributions and the regime of distributions, according to matter, space, time, and people (Pregno 2011, p. 55).

> *In the image and likeness of a salesperson in a business, in placing on the store counter, as a separate merchandise, the different possibilities of interpretation of the established rules; the politician, as a client and a buyer, acquires any of them according to the mysterious rules of motivation of the human act. These inscrutable rules hide the motivation of justice* (Goldschmidt, 1985, p. 386).

The theoretical contribution reviewed in these pages seeks to incorporate the compression of diachronic time within the General Theory of Law, so that Law does not go after the changes -successive or synchronic- but accompanies them with its structure -diachronically- without dikelogically dissolving the ideal -intelligible- *versus* the real -sensitive-.

In this way we also intend to hierarchize the objective understanding of the value justice with which Goldschmidt built his theory (Goldschmidt, 1958) and Maliandi supports his own (Maliandi; 1991), because if the Law with all its structure as a whole accompanies reality, the norm, values and time, justice does not become a temporary "construct" because in that case it depends on the observer -at a given moment- and not on the time that develops the value towards its true discovery.

This, although the observer sees in a synchronic way the present -"now"- is only a stage in full succession that has a movement -diachronically- taking the multidisciplinary ideas already manifested, that the dynamics of the processes is expressed by the correlations between the physical variables -visual, phenomenal, subjective of the observer- instead of the evolution of these with respect to time.

Thought of in Heideggerian terms, each "later" or "earlier" can be determined by starting with "now". The tendency to push the complete time in a present, which makes it go out of itself - as long as time is not defined as the time of the clock-, does not allow to wait that we arrive at the original sense (Heidegger, 1951). This can be in the fact that, being oriented to the future, it "pre-directs" to a sure but indeterminate perfection, which the Law has the imperative to direct, by the own original social character already raised of the discipline (Banchio, 2018a).

5.2 Contributions to Dikelogical Law

Without analyzing in detail, the diverse meanings that are usually assigned to structuralist theories, we will take advantage of them to simply allude to two general juridical structures that, as we already indicated, allow to be discerned with enough clarity: the synchronic structure designates the opposition between the universal and the particular -or individual- while the diachronic designates the opposition between permanence and change (Banchio, 2018a, p. 238).

In order for these general opposites, which have interested philosophical thought since its beginnings, to acquire, for example, for Maliandi, a conflictive character, it is necessary to understand them within the framework of dynamic systems such as the change of era, that is to say, it is also necessary to introduce the concept of strategies (Ciuro Caldani, 2011a), or - if it is a question of the dikelogical dimension - of "demanding duties" or relations of opposition and value preferences (Goldschmidt, 1985; Banchio, 2009).

According to Saussure, time has paradoxical effects on the specific entities that make up a system (Saussure, 1984). It is in the light of these temporospatial circumstances and the distributions of the sociological dimension in them, that the normative senses of the normological dimension are adapted.

This tends, in some way, to the universal, to the general validity of the law through the norm, and only in this sense does it clash -or diverge- with what tends to the admission or recognition of the individual, unique, unrepeatable of the sociological dimension. That conflict made visible as a potential or actual clash between the universal and the individual is "synchronic" because it does not involve "vital courses" of time (Ciuro Caldani, 1992, p. 25-28). Although the individual always develops in time, it is confronted with the universal - claim of validity of the normological face - in every instant, regardless of that development.

Conflict is "diachronic", on the other hand, when the temporal reference is constitutive as it seems to be happening in the change of era. It could also be thought that the change is made in time, while the permanence resists time; but the case is that the opposition itself consists in that difference (Maliandi; 2010).

The instances in conflict are precisely because of a before and an after: the opposing tendencies are that which points to the chronological posterior being equal to the anterior -that is, legal and therefore fair, or regulated by norms-, and that which points to the posterior being different from the anterior -changes or reforms in the normological dimension and in the evaluation of this and the distributions. Diachrony is present in the necessary reference to the passage from one to the other. Moreover, the "permanence" of something only makes sense in turn as a mode of temporal course: the always relative non-change requires the contrast with what, simultaneously, is changing, is, for Maliandi, in Bergsonian terms, "to remain", a mode of duration (Maliandi; 2010).

Specifying a characteristic with respect to foundational structuralism, these conflicts between the universal and the individual, on the one hand, and between permanence and change, on the other - between the respective tendencies - Maliandi calls them "intra-structural" to distinguish them from the conflicts between the instances of different structures, which are "inter- structural", but which, as we shall see, have much less importance, shaping, however, a sufficiently complex and multifaceted subject so that it can be approached, this time, from a different perspective.

5.3 Diachronic Axiology

Just as for Saussure it is the passage of time combined with social force that prevents the language from being a mere convention that can be modified by the interested parties, we think the same can be said for the justice of the Goldschmidtian dikelogical dimension.

That is why justice as a "construct" could not be thought of as valid, since its objectivity could only be ascertained through the passage of time that transforms into unjust valuations previously attributed as legal, *ex multis*, to slavery, racial segregation, inequality of women, animal cruelty, etc. Nevertheless, even so, the valuation as just or unjust of an adjudication - dikelogical dimension- requires a juridical community in whose framework the order is created -normological dimension- since it is not autonomous with respect to society -sociological dimension- that the *Tetrahedron* of Law[25] would unify precisely with the temporal dimension that allows this opposition within the unity that this figure, which would represent the juridical world, symbolizes.

The transfer of this idea to the speculative field of the General Theory of Law implies thinking of diachrony as subsidiary to synchrony and, therefore, as a tool whose contribution is limited to facilitating the understanding of a state from the description of how it has been reached, but what is absent, and what has been replaced. Diachrony would thus not have a fixed object as synchrony does. The state of the legal system is

---

[25] Figure of a Platonic solid, taken as a basis to exemplify the incorporation of space-time into the integral consideration of the juridical world (Banchio, 2018b).

observable and analyzable while change over time is simply a continuous flow (Lell, 2015a, p. 3-33; Lell, 2015b, p. 1-22).

The system is not perceived but a series of successive modifications and that is what would allow the Law to come from the "future", as the manifest changes of the present new Era demand. The question of synchrony and diachrony as profound possibilities and not only as fractions allows us to better understand the temporal development that is one of the most significant approaches of our figure of the *"tetrahedron"* (Banchio, 2018b) since the existence of interrelated synchronic and diachronic perspectives shows precisely the pantonomy of "possibility" (Ciuro Caldani, 1992, p. 25-28).

The diachronic perspective, if it is presented as secondary or relegated to a second level, is because it would not be able to contribute in "scientific" terms since its postulates would be descriptive of changes and of the future in terms of the replacement of one element by another. In this sense, if the scientific from the modern perspective is measured from the enunciation of explanatory laws with vocation of generality and causality, the juridical diachrony fails (Lell, 2015a, p. 3-33). If it is not possible to predict changes, identify relationships of cause and effect and provide explanations with a vocation for universality, the Law will continue to lag the different post-modern strategies that today postpone it.

Although in the legal field, synchronic states have similar characteristics, their delimitation is difficult since there are always changes, some of greater importance, others more irrelevant, but it is necessary to abstract them to conceive an idea of a static legal order during a certain period. The relevance of these changes is conventionally defined and constitutes a simplification that tends to reduce a wide *phenomenon* to an approachable instance (Lell, 2015a, p. 3- 33).

Synchrony specializes in the arrangement of time and space. Diachrony, on the other hand, goes back in time and projects itself on it, analyzes both the past and the future possibilities around the meanings of a normative formulation. It does not involve any kind of cutbacks, since it requires the search for the roots of prescription without being limited to a particular order or a limited period of validity (Lell, 2015a, p. 3-33).

As Ciuro Caldani points out, in the dikelogical dimension, diachrony means a strong integration of justice with other values, especially for the author, usefulness, to such an extent that the relationship of means and ends can lead to the excess in which some are simply justified by others. However, the utility that is linked to diachrony supposes an important reference to the ends. The change of era presented by Postmodernity lives above all a utility "of means", which has mostly a synchronic character. The synchronic perspective is more related to justice of departure, while diachrony is more linked to justice of arrival. The synchrony refers more to the "defraction" of the justice influences of other distributions, of the complex and of the consequences, while the diachrony attends more to the "defraction" of the justice influences of the past and the future (Ciuro Caldani, 1992, p. 27).

Therefore, the special use that we can give to it for the postulation of both kinds of justice of the future, which will give the law the possibility to take the lead in future changes with a legal strategy.

In this sense, it is useful to consider the dikelogical assessments around two axes as those proposed in this work, on the one hand, around the relationships that exist with the other dimensions of the system, that is, with the elements that are simultaneously present in the system and together with which their dikelogical senses are mutually determined, and, on the other hand, in relation to the temporal succession of the same element towards the past and towards the future anticipating how those states are modified, what changes from one state to another and how the variation of the elements impacts on the system in general constitute the object of diachrony in law.

The excessive synchronic perspective, that is the "dispersion", usually leads to the non-humanist overflow of individualism, in which the subject takes others as means, while the excessive diachronic perspective, that is the "obsession", can lead to the non-humanist overflow of totalitarianism, that in the interest of the pursued ends, the individuals are mediated. A just regime, therefore, must protect the individual from both "dispersion" and "obsession"[26].

6. Classes of Diachronic Justice

As we saw above, the objectivity of justice is evident to Goldschmidt in that the just solution to each case is one. For this reason, the diversity of types of justice developed by Ciuro Caldani shows us different paths to the discovery of that one solution, and they at least seek impartiality in the form

---

[26] The names of the objects that do not share the excessive synchrony and diachrony are "tardiness" and "haste" respectively. (Ciuro Caldani, 1992, p. 25).

of the adjudication -precedent path- since a neutral evaluation is impossible, because, as we also pointed out above, the subjective aspects are inevitably intermingled in the evaluations of the objectivity of justice.

But the complexity does not end with this since those classes were only seen statically and we do not yet have the movement incorporated in the diversity of the assessments of justice as a deep possibility of understanding the just solution of the case and not only as part of the fractions with which the original trialism had already foreseen them in a masterful way (Goldschmidt, 1985; Banchio, 2009, p. 84).

This is achieved in a significant way if the theoretical approaches of the justice classes allow a better understanding of the temporal development within their classification. Independently of the orientations, with which can be represented the courses of time and the senses of our lives -right, semi right, circumferences or concentric circles-, it is given to use the two basic perspectives of comprehension of the classes of justice as we already saw, a "synchronic" one, that is centered in the simultaneity of the phenomena and another "diachronic" one, that mainly refers to its successive character (Ciuro Caldani, 1988, p. 25).

However, these two phenomena are also interrelated. What follows is not a play on words for Maliandi, but an attempt to show that it is easier to operate with two *phenomena* -multiplicity- than with one -unit-. We will use for it, once again, an example taken from Maliandi, for whom it is understandable the statement that, from a diachronic point of view, multiplicity is a simultaneous change; but the authentic changes are successive changes (Maliandi, 2010, p. 92).

Similarly, unity can be thought of diachronically as a simultaneous permanence, although, strictly speaking, the permanence must also be durable, that is, successive. Viewed from the synchronic side, change could be defined as a successive multiplicity, but this is easily distinguishable from a simultaneous multiplicity-the experience of seeing many things at the same time-for example, a school of fish does not have much in common with the experience of seeing one thing in different stages-for example, a fish that becomes fish and then flour or oil, and so on. And, no doubt, and even with rhetorical or didactic benefit, one could define permanence as successive unity; but we still understand that one thing is to observe that a certain fish remains a fish -no one caught it- and another, clearly discernible, is to observe the unity of this fish, which is one and not a shoal (Maliandi, 2010, p. 93).

On the other hand, unity can be linked to change: something unitary can be replaced by another instance also unitary, with which there is change - "successive multiplicity" or diachronic difference- without synchronic multiplicity -example: a president ends his term of office and another assumes that position, he succeeds him - and a multiplicity can be linked to permanence, in the case of a set of things that remain identical over time, with which there will be "successive unity" - as we saw, a metaphor for permanence -, that is, diachronic identity, without synchronic unity - for example: a cabinet of ministers - different from each other, and perhaps even conflicting - that remains unchanged throughout a period of government[27].

To better understand the above, we will resort to the cinema, as a mere example of apparent movement perception -"synchronic and diachronic"- which also reveals the co-participation of the two factors discussed above - "subjective and objective"-.

As it is known, static pictures are projected on the screen; if such pictures follow each other at a certain speed, we do not see static pictures but moving ones. A spectator who is not aware of the mechanism of the perception of apparent movement will find it difficult to admit that the rapid "movements" of the dancer before his eyes, of the wheels of the car, or the legs of the running horse, which he "sees" on the screen, are the result of his own contribution. In turn, whoever discovered the contribution of the subject, could commit the error of axiological subjectivism, and affirm that all that we see is a mere projection of the subject. We could also speak of different timelines, where each one would be a fractal of another greater timeline and justice would be "predictive", if as quantum theory maintains seen above the objective measurement of time depends on the

---

[27] This range of possibilities, which can hardly be hinted at here, is in Maliandi's view the main reason why it is necessary to distinguish (without ignoring their mutual relations) the two synchronic and diachronic structures. For the author cited, it was Henri Bergson (1859-1941) who perceived this type of confusion and denounced it in his peculiar metaphysics of consciousness, when he distinguished between "duration" and "objective" time. The latter, spatially measurable (through the representation of a line, the movement of the hands of the clock or the trajectory of a star in the celestial sphere), has to be distinguished from that one, in a similar way as we should distinguish the diachronic from the synchronic (Maliandi, 1991, p. 93).

observer and never on the agent who moves in time (Panchelyuga and Shnoll, 2007, p. 51).

The truth is that the contribution of the subject allows us to see the object in movement, but if the static images were not projected there would be no perception. Perception in cinema is the synthesis of a double contribution: static images constitute the objective aspect and movement is added by the subject (Frondizi, 1968, p. 152). Something similar happens with justice, which is also the synthesis of subjective reactions to qualities that are appreciated in the object, to which the dynamics of synchronic simultaneity and diachronic succession in movement must be added (Ciuro Caldani, 1982/4, p. 62).

Let us see then if we can now, - in the light of the ideas of distributive and corrective justice of Aristotle (1972), the classes of justice of the distributions and the regime of Ciuro Caldani (2007, p. 36) and taking advantage of Saussure's anticipated contributions to explain the classification from the dynamic point of view, of the guiding and corrective justice, of departure, arrival and procedure (Rawls, 1986; Ciuro Caldani, 1987, p. 715; 2007), of criticism and construction (Ciuro Caldani, 1987).

6.1 Governing and corrective justice

In the above direction we can distinguish a basic governing (guiding) justice, which is shown in relation to the maintenance or development of what is just, and another correcting justice, which -as its name indicates- "straightens out" or "corrects" the injustices (Ciuro Caldani, 1982/4, p. 62).

For example, when a contract is concluded, it can be assumed that the governing (guiding) justice intervenes; but when services are interrupted, the imbalance - "divalence" - of powers and powers requires the intervention of the corrective justice. The same thing happens, for example, when a crime has occurred and the penalty must be applied, even though at times justice may intervene at the beginning or the end, as we shall see below (e.g., pardons).

The two kinds of justice referred to are permanent needs, because the dynamics of the world provoke changing situations of justice and injustice. With a view to their coincidence, the idea of "constantly renewed justice" (Ciuro Caldani, 1982/4, p. 62) is particularly enlightening.

6.2 Justice of departure, arrival, and processing

To be complete, the right thing to do must be discovered by recognizing how the case must be solved according to its current reality - in its starting situation - and what the result of the solution must be with a view to a better world - in its arrival situation. To these perspectives, dynamic by reference, we should add the perspective of procedural justice, in which the dynamic is in the way of establishing what must be done. The perspective of formality can refer to the departure or the arrival, recognizing the tension between both, or be radicalized to the extent of limiting itself to having as just what has been established by the path that is considered due, so that the way of establishing what is just eclipses the reference to what has to be discovered. In truth, procedural justice is an element of justice of departure or arrival, taken from another point of view also dynamic, but it can end up overflowing monopolizing the consideration of what is just (Ciuro Caldani, 1987, p. 716).

To avoid this, the synchronic approach to justice must be integrated with the already mentioned dynamism of diachronic understanding, with respect to departure and arrival and also of the procedure. The synchronic perspective is more related to the justice "of departure"; on the other hand, the diachrony is more related to the justice "of arrival" (Ciuro Caldani, 1992, p. 25-26)

The example mentioned by Ciuro Caldani, in the case of homicide, the demands concerning the situation in which the dead man and the killer were found and the grounds for or against the killer's action constitute the starting point; the demands concerning what is to result from the solution so that a better world may emerge - which may include a pardon, for example - make for the justice of arrival, and the demands concerning how to establish what is to be done with the killer belong to the justice of procedure. While justice is one, and by deepening each perspective full justice must be found, due consideration of departure, arrival and proceeding favors understanding (Ciuro Caldani, 1987, p. 716).

In a certain sense, however, special attention must be given to the arrival, because the departure and the procedure are integrated with greater clarity in the full reference to the arrival and because in this way the axiological expansion and the leading role of man is better served, mainly in the culmination of the temporal event. Now that the end of man can be the work of man, and that we can change basic realities with amazing scope - genetics is opening revolutionary possibilities - the interest in justice of arrival is more urgent and must be greater. Justice will increasingly be the construction of a better world and not the correction of a reality that will be formed in growing dependence on our will (Ciuro Caldani, 1987, p. 717).

6.3 Critical and constructive justice

Closely linked to the understanding of the references of justice to departure and arrival is the recognition of two paths of justice especially linked to one and the other: critical justice and justice of construction. If, on the departure side, justice has a frequent sense of discontent, of negative reference and oriented towards reform, on the arrival side it has a sense of aspiration, of positive reference and oriented towards creation. Justice is criticism and reform of the existing world, but also construction, creation of a new world, and this is the ultimate meaning of progress (Ciuro Caldani, 1987, p. 720).

Post-modernity, which like every change of era implies a profound transformation of values, presents a justice of criticism of "negative values" that are not part of the justice of construction of the new civilization, e.g., racism, warmongering, *"machismo"*, patriotism, ideological and religious fundamentalism, slavery, sexism, hatred, exclusion, *aporophobia*, therapeutic poisoning, contamination and of "false manufactured values" such as that of the artificial paradise of drugs (Banchio, 2018a, p. 243).

On the other hand, justice in construction is based on a complex axiology of values such as fraternity, unity, integration, peace, forgiveness, truth, reconciliation, where having implies sharing, knowing how not to impose, ordering to serve - power as service -, solidarity with the world, the environment, the neighbor, the companion, ex multis, where the one who believes is contagious.

In a critical sense, justice in law is linked to the silence of the victims of violence, who can no longer cry out, especially the innocent and defenseless; it defends, with its awards, the families who are in difficulty, and who mourn the tragic loss of their children, it protects all people who suffer from hunger, in a world that, on the other hand, allows itself the luxury of throwing away tons of food every day. It punishes the traffickers who cause the suffering of mothers and fathers who see their children fall victim to drug abuse and profit from it. With the justice of construction, it joins those who are persecuted because of their religion, their ideas, or simply because of the color of their skin or sexual condition and appears to sanction the selfishness and corruption in political institutions that leads so many young people to lose confidence in the construction of a better world.

6.4 The frontiers of justice

As the vocation of totality is a general characteristic of the paradigms of justice (Ciuro Caldani, 2007, p. 79), pantonomy demands cuts that are translated with different degrees in "borders" of justice, which claims to know what could have been and what can still be in the discovery of its objectivity -not neutrality-[28]. Depending on the characteristics of the cutting lines, these more or less permeable or impermeable "borders" are produced (Ciuro Caldani, 2007, p. 79).

> *One of the greatest channels for increasing one's own possibilities of distribution is to take possession of the situational frameworks to define the borders, since he who writes history, writes the future.* (Ciuro Caldani, 2007, p. 85).

In the justice of departure, its "corrective" deployment predominates and in the justice of arrival the "governing (guiding)" projection will predominate. When considering "corrective" justice, it must be recognized that it is never possible to totally "correct" the deviations of a starting situation, mainly because never two moments are equivalent, so it is necessary to be on guard against the risks of wanting to correct everything or of the discouragement that leads to not correcting anything (Ciuro Caldani, 1987, p. 720).

In turn, when considering "governing" (guiding) justice, we must warn that it is never possible to rule everything, because what is realized is always more complex than what is projected, so we must be attentive to the utopian deviations that want to lead everything and the abandonment deviations, which do not want to rule anything (Banchio, 2018a, p. 244).

The adjudication of criminal and civil responsibility must consider the inherent limits of corrective justice, and the models that are elaborated to build the future must above all take into account the limits of guiding justice, only in this way will justice be increasingly the construction of a

---

[28] Goldschmidt (1987, p. 114) refers to the knowledge provided by the method of the variations that imaginatively modify the case, its possible solutions and the means to reach them, recognizing the "socio-normic-dikelogic" points of view, that Ciuro Caldani has used to "cut" the borders of justice (Ciuro Caldani, 2007).

better world and not the criticism of "departure" situations (Ciuro Caldani, 1987, p. 720).

7. Bottom line

As we stated in the Introduction, the Law has to "come" from the "to come", because otherwise the social demand makes it a discipline "a la carte" of the satisfaction of specific social needs behind the decisions taken by other areas, ignoring the strong sense of future of the Law whose rules must contain not only "promises" that something "will be", but "prescriptions" of something that must be, especially for the realization of justice of arrival, for a better world that "must be" (Ciuro Caldani, 2011, p. 96).

Things happen in social reality and the Law captures those realities that benefit or harm life through its ex post facto normative formulation, to provide it with the sense of justice, whose realization it intends to carry out and is the distinctive feature of the Law, which distinguishes it from any other discipline.

This requires the Law to take advantage of the opportunities for the realization of that ex ante justice with an objective character and confronts it with the problem of decision making because otherwise it will continue to be in the rearguard of genetics, robotics or the market, seeing itself as impossible to develop "anticipatory" legal responses.

To comply with this requirement, legal discipline over time must seek the diachronic realization of its three ontological components.

The diachronic classes of justice, with a sense of future "progress", guiding and correcting, of criticism and construction and of departure, of procedure and arrival are the best way to understand the characteristics of the future - temporal dimension - for a better world than the "must be" of Law - dikelogical dimension - starting from the current "being" with the indicators of the present reality - sociological dimension - through the capture of norms - normological dimension - can establish with a sense of legal strategy towards the future. This is in order not to lose the leading role that law has always had in Western culture and which it should not renounce, if it integrates it with the complexity of the figure with self-conjugated unity of the *tetrahedron* that we use to signify it.

Trialism from its original formulation, with the objectivity of the value of justice and the deepening of its developments through the theory of legal answers, the dynamic understanding of social reality and justice, the general theory of common and comprehensive law and the legal strategy offers the enriching conceptual possibilities for this to happen, incorporating the "future" time, taking into account the indicators of the present, for an objective justice of arrival for a better world as a possibility of providing those legal answers, *ex multis*, to the singularity, the artificial intelligence, inclusive robotics, of which the Law, we insist, seems to be behind.

To this conceptual richness of Juristics we add in these meditations the contributions of the consideration of time in its most current conceptual formulations, based on hypotheses of the quantum physics theory (Rovelli, 2014) that the dynamics of processes is expressed by the correlations between physical variables, instead of the evolution of these with respect to time, which allows us to argue favorably, as we have explained, to sustain the objectivity of the value of justice with which the founder of Trialism developed his theory, although detached in this case from the ontological and metaphysical bases that gave it origin.

Conclusion

The change of era, which places man in front of the management of his own species and, where "being" became simply " to be", brought a logic of transformations that was unprecedented as the present culmination of Western history, both because of the intensity and because of the speed and depth of the changes that occur at an accelerated rate in an exponential curve, since each one is greater than the previous one and the next one even more so. Disenchanted with Umberto Eco's ideal of modernity for the "apocalyptic man of culture", the notions of space and time are a universe of immediacy, where sequential or chronological time is diluted and where physical space begins to be irrelevant.

The legal system anchored to a syllogistic past with a General Theory developed as a memory load of the previous doctrines, a memory that is reiterated again, leaves the Law anchored to an "agrarian" past that keeps its legal responses lagging technological advances, since its role is generally reactive and late, and it does not manage to "synchronize" its evolution with the rhythm that technological innovations acquire.

The conclusion of the contribution of Doctoral Thesis to which we made repeated reference in these three of this book is the profound innovation in the field of the General Theory of Law, within the theoretical framework of the Trialist theory of incorporating time as one more essential dimension of the Legal World, taking as a basis the "temporospatial" idea that physics offers in the quantum theoretical conceptions that we have expressed in it, since time and space visibly compressed, can be taken advantage of by Law.

To illustrate this, in the reference work, we have taken from geometry, the idea of the "3-simplex", a convex envelope of a set of points with no more than one plane containing them and encompassing them all, through a four-sided polyhedron - *tetrahedron* - including the three dimensions and the time of future changes that the present shows us and the legal past tries to respond as a way of expressing the avant-garde that "law must come from the future" and not remain in its rear. Although the "4.0" pattern is still marketing without a market standard - legaltech - the four faces also symbolise it in the possible direction towards "hypermodernity".

This thought and figure schematise our doctrinal contribution of avoiding the synchronic succession that, in the face of the disruptive changes that are taking place in one "face" of the law - sociological dimension -, another of its "faces" - nomological dimension - arrives later, like the flight of the Minerva's owl pointed out by Hegel[29], and the third - justice - is a merely constructed assessment producing injustices - Maliandi's "identity-difference" conflict.

That is why the incorporation of a temporary "face" by adapting the teachings of the Maliandi, Doctor of Mainz, as a successive multiplicity linked to the change of Law -successive unit- (Maliandi, 2010, pp. 92-93), so that he, in a diachronic way, accompanies the change of era, conserving his future protagonism and his role of saying not only what "should be" but what will be, always consecrating justice as the main and distinctive characteristic of our discipline.

The factual application of the hypotheses is validated in the accelerated advance of human "creations" that do not have a previous regulatory legal framework and present the Law with normative and axiological difficulties even once they have been produced.

---

[29] Most of the translations were made from the Italian version by Francesco Messineo, so, as we have already done with Goethe's work, it is appropriate to reproduce the German text, as it can be translated differently: *"Um noch über das Belehren, wie die Welt sein soll, ein Wort zu sagen, so kommt dazu ohnehin die Philosophie immer zu spät. Als der Gedanke der Welt erscheint sie erst in der Zeit, nachdem die Wirklichkeit ihren Bildungsprozeß vollendet und sich fertig gemacht hat. Dies, was der Begriff lehrt, zeigt notwendig ebenso die Geschichte, daß erst in der Reife der Wirklichkeit das Ideale dem Realen gegenüber erscheint und jenes sich dieselbe Welt, in ihrer Substanz erfaßt, in Gestalt eines intellektuellen Reichs erbaut. Wenn die Philosophie ihr Grau in Grau malt, dann ist eine Gestalt des Lebens alt geworden, und mit Grau in Grau läßt sie sich nicht verjüngen, sondern nur erkennen; die Eule der Minerva beginnt erst mit der einbrechenden Dämmerung ihren Flug".* (Hegel, 1966, pp. 9-10).

To this end, we exemplify the dynamic categories of justice of the future within our "spatial" theoretical conception of the continental legal system with the broad development that we have shown "temporarily" throughout philosophy, from its Greek origins.

We consider that this model of legal strategy of inclusion of time is preferable to the "predictive justice" of artificial intelligence, blockchain, big data or crowdjury that postulates an economicist strategic model eager for research and the advances that it is exponentially achieving, for which the Law in its current doctrinally majority conceptions, does not find anticipatory answers and only does so ex post facto.

Legal responses are always after the facts and reality demonstrates what the visionary of the "global village" Mc Luhman states, that many looks at the future through the rearview mirror and believe they are heading towards the future, when in fact they are repeating the past.

References

Aristotle (1972). *Etica Nicomaquea*. Trad. P. de Azcárate. Madrid: Epasa-Calpe.

Banchio, P. (2007). "Metodología jurídica trialista". *Dos Filosofías del derecho argentinas anticipatorias. Homenaje a Werner Goldschmidt y a Carlos Cossio*. Rosario: Fundación para las Investigaciones Jurídicas, 13-26.

Banchio, P. (2009). *La noción trialista del derecho* (2° ed.). Buenos Aires: Perspectivas Jurídicas.

Banchio, P. (2018a). *Desarrollos Trialistas*. Buenos Aires: Perspectivas Jurídicas.

Banchio, P. (2018b). *El tetraedro del Derecho. Aportes para una Teoría General del Derecho Privado Trialista*, agosto de 2018, Unpublished.

Banchio, P. (2018c). "Consideraciones iusfilosóficas para una nueva dimensión en la Teoría General del Derecho". *Doctrina Jurídica*, 20, 3-47.

Banchio, P. (2018d). "Notas sobre los aportes teóricos para una dimensión integradora en la Teoría General del Derecho". *Ratio Iuris VI* (2), 49-104.

Banchio, P. (2020). "Contributions to the objective character of the value justice from the synchrony and diachrony and the concept of quantum time". *Metaphilosophy eJournal*, Vol 12, Issue 6, May 21, 2020, 1-21. Viewed at: http://ssrn.com/abstract= 3576147.

Bianchi, D. (2015a). "Il tempo non esiste". Viewed at: http://www.fisicisenzapalestra.com/filosofia/il-tempo-non-esiste/ March 5, 2015.

Bianchi, D. (2015b). "Vi presento Anassimandro". Viewed at: https://www.fisicisenzapalestra.com/filosofia/anassimandro/ January 18, 2015.

Ciuro Caldani, M. A. (1982/84). *Estudios de Filosofía Jurídica y Filosofía política*. Rosario: Fundación para las Investigaciones Jurídicas.

Ciuro Caldani, M. A. (1987). "Hacia una comprensión dinámica de la justicia (justicia y progreso)". *El Derecho,* 123, 715-721.

Ciuro Caldani, M. A. (1988). "La Filosofía, el trialismo y nuestra situación de espacio y tiempo". *Investigación y Docencia,* 5, 3-7.

Ciuro Caldani, M. A. (1992). "Significados jusfilosóficos de los cursos vitales". *Investigación y Docencia,* 19, 25-28.

Ciuro Caldani, M. A. (2007). *Metodología dikelógica*. Rosario: Fundación para las Investigaciones Jurídicas.

Ciuro Caldani, M. A. (2011). *Estrategia Jurídica*. Rosario: UNR Editora.

Ciuro Caldani, M. A. (2019). *Una teoría Trialista del mundo jurídico*, Rosario: FDER Editora.

Diez Blanco, A. (1960). *La filosofía y sus problemas*. Barcelona: Scientia.

Frondizi, R. (1968). *¿Qué son los valores?* México: Fondo de Cultura Económica.

Goldschmidt, W. (1958). *La ciencia de la justicia (Dikelogía)*. Madrid: Aguilar.

Goldschmidt, W. (1985). *Introducción filosófica al derecho*. Buenos Aires: Depalma.

Greco, P. (2014). "Il tempo è un'illusione, per quanto tenace. Il giornale dell'Universitá degli studi di Padova". Viewed at: http://www.unipd.it/ilbo/content/il-tempo-e-un%E2%80%99 illusione-quanto-tenace.

Hartmann, N. (1962). *Ethik* (4° Aufl.). Berlin: W. de Gruyter.

Hawking, S. (1987). *Breve Historia del Tiempo*. Madrid: Alianza.

Hegel, G. W. F. (1966). *Fenomenología del espíritu*. Trad. de W. Roces. México: Fondo de Cultura Económica.

Heidegger, M. (1951). *Was ist Metaphysik*. Frankfurt am Main: Vittorio Klostermann.

Lell, H. (2015a). "Un modelo "saussureano" de la ciencia del derecho en torno a la dicotomía sincronía/diacronía: afirmaciones y críticas en paralelo con la lingüística". *Revista Telemática de Filosofía del Derecho*, 2015, 18. 3-33.

Lell, H. (2015b). "Diacronía y sincronía de los sentidos normativos constitucionales. Algunas posibles intervenciones semánticas". *Cartapacio de Derecho,* 27, 1-22.

Madile, J. (2007). *La muerte del sentido*. Rosario: UNR.

Maliandi, R. (1991). *Ética: conceptos y problemas*. Buenos Aires: Biblos.

Maliandi, R. (2010). *Ética Convergente*, "Fenomenología de la conflictividad". (Tomo I). Buenos Aires: Las Cuarenta.

Panchelyuga, V. A., y Shnoll, S. E. (2007). "On the dependence of local-time effects on spatial direction". *Progress in Physics, 2007*(3), 51–54.

Pregno, E. (2011). "La metodologización de la dikelogía en el pensamiento de Miguel Ángel Ciuro Caldani". *Cartapacio de Derecho*, 20, 1-66.

Rawls, J. (1986). *Teoría de la Justicia*. México: Fondo de Cultura Económica.

Rovelli, C. (2014). *Che cos'è il tempo? Che cos'è lo spazio?* Roma: Di Renzo.

Rovelli, C. (2016). *Siete breves lecciones de Física*. Trad. J. Ramos Mena. Madrid: Anagrama.

Saussure, F. (1984). *Curso de lingüística general*. Trad. A. Alonso. Buenos Aires: Losada.

Scheler, M. (1948). *Ética*. Buenos Aires: Revista de Occidente.

St. Thomas (1966). *Suma Teológica*. Madrid: B.A.C.

Zucchi, H. (2001). *El derecho como objeto tridimensional*. Córdoba: Academia Nacional de Derecho y Ciencias Sociales de Córdoba.

About the Author

Pablo Rafael Banchio (Current CV)

Education

- PhD in Law (Orientation in Private Law), University of Business and Social Sciences (UCES).
- Magister in Business Law, Universidad Austral (UA) and its equivalents to Laurea in Giurisprudenza and Biennale University Master, qualifying all'insegnamento di Diritto Impresariale in Italy (MAE.IT).
- Specialist in Business Legal Advice, University of Buenos Aires (UBA)
- Postdoctorate in Fundamental Principles and Human Rights (UCES).

Positions
- Director of the Master in Business Law at the University of Business and Social Sciences (UCES).
- Professor of Doctorate: General Theory of Law (UCES) and Intensive Doctorate (UNR), Methodology of Research (UNLaM), Epistemology (UCES) and Fintech, Blockchain and cryptocurrencies (UCES).
- Professor of Master: Finance, Banking and Financial Law, Business Ethics and Business Legal Advice and Compliance and Internal Control (UCES) and Judicial Interpretation in Master in Magistracy (UBA).
- Professor of the Updating Program: Constitutional Law in Human Rights and Integration Law (UBA).
- Professor of degree: Philosophy of Law and Law of Financial Markets (UCES).

Research
- External Researcher in the research project "Economic Analysis of Law and the Judicial System in Argentina", in the Academic Department Graduate School in the Program: CyTMA2, National University of La Matanza (UNLaM).
- Presentation to the "Visiting researchers' program on the Faculty of Law" (UBA) for the area of International Humanitarian Law within the framework of the Postdoctoral program in Law.
- "Scientific Programming" on the Faculty of Philosophy within the framework of the Postdoctoral program in Philosophy

Publications
- Author of 15 books, 5 parts of books, 55 papers and 9 university fascicles.

Composed, assembled and designed by **Forum Accademico** in November 2020. Printed and bound in Buenos Aires (Argentine)

www.ingramcontent.com/pod-product-compliance
Lightning Source LLC
Chambersburg PA
CBHW070808220526
45466CB00002B/596